D1522490

THE SPIRITUAL MEANINGS OF NUMBERS

HOW TO EMBRACE THE SYNCHRONICITIES OF ANGEL NUMBERS AND ACHIEVE THE MAGIC OF MANIFESTATION

BELLE MOTLEY

CONTENTS

A Free Gift for You!

In the **"Vibe Guide,"** you will learn...

- **15** techniques to raise your vibrations and stay in a high frequency

- How to manifest your desires

- How to find peace...

and so much more!

Go to bellemotley.com to receive your free gift!

Or scan the QR code!

INTRODUCTION

Have you ever walked alone down a country lane at night? Around you, the trees and bushes are blanketed in shadows. Perhaps, far off in the distance, you can catch the pinprick gold of a farmhouse's windows? All that you can hear is your footsteps, the rustle of grass, and the creaking of trees.

Above you, a grand vista spreads—the glimmer of the Milky Way with its array of countless stars. On a summer day, it feels so close. You want to try to reach up and touch it, but you know that each one of those pinpricks is light-years away.

The vastness of space feels overwhelming, mainly because we are all subconsciously trying to cope with the big questions we face in life in our daily lives. When we allow the vastness of the Universe to sink in, we can explore our vulnerability and seeming insignificance.

Perhaps you have felt these moments during other periods of your life: When you face unemployment, when a loved one passes away, or when natural disasters hit. Anxiety and stress may overwhelm you until you feel like you have no way out. During these moments, you may feel lost and alone in an uncaring Universe... but are you?

I have something to tell you: You are not alone. You are cared for and loved. You have a destiny. You matter. Now, are you ready to see it?

OPENING THE DOOR

There is something else you may have experienced recently, perhaps something you have noticed. Numbers keep popping up wherever you go. These numbers are always the same repeating numbers.

For example, maybe you ride the Number 14 bus to work. Then, you notice that your credit card statement is $1414.00. Your mother lives on the 14th floor of her apartment building. What is going on? Are these just coincidences? Or are the number patterns happening for a reason? What could they be saying?

These two experiences—vulnerability and coincidence—are an invitation to re-evaluate our lives, goals, and values, as well as our notions about reality. One response would be to dismiss these feelings and return our focus to "the real world" on "what matters." However, there is another way to explore these feelings and experiences: Embracing the guides of the Universe, your angels, and leveraging the power of numerology to manifest your dreams.

MEET BELLE MOTLEY

My name is Belle Motley, and I know where you are coming from. When I was a child, I was fascinated with numbers. This fascination led me to numerology, and although I was familiar with this form of spiritual guidance, I never appreciated the power of Angel Numbers until my mother passed away. With my mother's passing, I felt so alone. The Universe felt so uncaring and distant.

Then, I began to notice something strange happening. First, my mother's presence became real to me. Songs began to pop up on the radio—songs my mother used to sing to me in the car as a child. Sometimes, I could smell her perfume at night, just like when she used to tuck me into bed. I no longer felt alone because I knew my mother was with me. A reading from a medium confirmed my beliefs. As she made contact, the medium discovered that my mother was there to help me. All I needed to do was ask. Next, patterns of numbers started to appear around me. The clock. The TV. My bank balance. My phone. Even in my dreams. In more and more areas of my life, numbers repeated themselves to me.

Instead of ignoring them, my love for numbers encouraged me to research and explore why these synchronicities were happening. My research pointed me to numerology and the power of Angel Numbers. I no longer felt like the Universe was cold and far away.

After my mother's passing, I began to better understand and utilize numerology in my personal life. Not only did numerology enable me to analyze myself and recognize my destiny, but it reassured me that I was not alone. With contact from my angel guides, I received directions on pursuing my dreams and achieving my goals. As my mental health flourished, I was better positioned to increase my confidence, positivity, and success.

I am dreaming of the same for you. I want to help you achieve your dreams and goals through the proper use of Angel Numbers. I want you to know that you are not alone. I want you to recognize that things happen for a reason. I want you to know that you are important and that you have a unique destiny of your own to embrace.

I wrote this book for you.

LOOKING AHEAD

We will be entering a deep dive into numerology, Angel Numbers, the Law of Attraction, and manifestation in the coming chapters. Sounds exciting? Confusing? Strange? Don't worry! We will be exploring each facet of numerology step-by-step, defining what it is and how it can help you move forward in life with confidence.

In Chapter 1, we will be covering basic definitions and theories behind numerology. It will include explorations of Pythagorean numerology, the Fibonacci Sequence, and other numerology basics. We will then explore the general ideas and theories surrounding angel numbers in Chapter 2. Next, Chapters 3-5 will define and explain the meanings of specific numbers and number combinations, focusing on enabling you to learn how to interpret numbers for yourself. We will cover practical steps to connect with your angel numbers and show you how to respond to disconnection in Chapter 6. Chapter 7 holds the culmination of what we learned, focusing on manifestation and how to use angel numbers (and specific practical meditational techniques) to ensure success and peace of mind. Finally, as encouragement, I will share quotes, poetry, and prayers in Chapter 8, which you will hopefully find helpful during meditation or relaxation.

As you rediscover the energies of the cosmos, the love of our angel guides, and the power of angel numbers, you will be one step closer to self-acceptance, confidence, and success. The Universe is no longer far-off and empty. The road is no longer uncertain and directionless. The stars are speaking to you.

Let's get you started on your journey!

1

WHAT IS NUMEROLOGY?

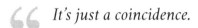 *It's just a coincidence.*

That's what friends and family would tell me when I began to notice a number popping up repeatedly: 222. What could it mean? Was it just a coincidence? I didn't believe so. I saw these numbers for a reason.

What if numbers meant more than simple value markers? What if they are alive in a way that we could never imagine? What if they are expressions of the interactive cosmos in which we live? How would our lives change if we could tap into the very framework of the Universe itself?

Numerology holds the answers to all of these questions—and more.

DEFINING NUMEROLOGY

From the beginning, humans have been obsessed with counting, ordering, and valuating. Throughout history, human curiosity has revealed numerological structures within the natural world. We have found mathematical patterns in seashells and human faces. Symmetry, seasons, and processional cycles all point to a numerical framework hidden in the cosmos. Numerology may not necessarily explain how these patterns came to be or who might have caused them. But it does note that numerical synchronicities exist within nature for a reason.

From the Kabbalah to Pagan spiritual traditions, numbers play a role in divination, self-actualization, and influence. In Kabbalah, for example, the numerical calculations hidden in one's name may hold particular significance. For Pagans, numbers have great spiritual value, though some can be more influential or powerful than others.

Numerology, in short, is utilizing numbers to identify one's destiny. Using particular calculations linked to your birthdate or name, you can identify themes, goals, or paths that will help you achieve a happier and more successful life. Besides your name and birthdate, numerology can help make sense of number patterns that appear to recur throughout your life.

Numerology has been around for a long time. However, one of the main figures known for formally formulating theories about numerology is Pythagoras, a famous Greek philosopher, and mathematician.

A figure of legend, not much is sure about Pythagoras. He was born in Greece around 570 BCE and founded a school in Croton (located in South Italy), where he taught math and philosophy. Pythagoras also attempted to formalize his theories about the structure of the Universe. Although many historical accounts are biased for or against Pythagoras, there are stories about his journeys and studies in Egypt and the Middle East. He learned ancient religions and cult secrets from the Egyptian priests and Babylonian/Chaldean Magi. As a result, Pythagoras's theories surrounding numerology were potentially based on ancient traditions.

Pythagoras and his students went on to make more discoveries and observations about the Universe and mathematics, resulting in the formulation of the famous Pythagorean Theorem, which we still use today. You probably recognize the Pythagorean Theorem. The formula is "the sum of the squares on the legs of a right triangle is equal to the square on the hypotenuse" (The Editors of Encyclopedia Britannica, 2018a). This mathematical discovery was the direct result of Pythagoras and his student's dedication to the study of numbers and numerical patterns in nature.

WHAT IS PYTHAGOREAN NUMEROLOGY?

As we just learned, numerology has been around for centuries, but it has been slowly cultivated in European culture thanks to Pythagoras. As a result, numerology is more often than not conflated with Pythagorean numerology. However, other forms of the concept existed and developed in the world before and concurrently with Pythagoras's theories.

Pythagoras's school theorized that everything in the cosmos is related to each other, and we can express this relationship through patterns of numbers. In short, Pythagorean numerology provided a way to uncover one's destiny through numerical forms of divination.

Numerologists today believe that the lost mystical knowledge Pythagoras utilized is still meaningful. Although many secrets have been obscured over time, our ability today to access information from around the globe about ancient civilizations and belief systems allows us to understand the broad scope of numerology better. Therefore, moving forward, we will be using the word 'numerology' as an inclusive term to allow for multiple readings and types of numerology beyond what Pythagoras theorized.

WHAT IS ENERGY?

We have established a few things so far: the Universe has structure, which we can express in numerical values. You can use these values to speak the truth about yourself, your world, and your future. However, it is essential to realize that numbers are not simply signposts but living parts of an ever-transforming Universe.

As a result, numbers are intrinsically tied to energy. Since energy and vibrations can affect the way you experience life, numbers can also affect yourself and your experiences. Recent theories on consciousness and reality suggest that perhaps the formation of life and awareness as we experience it today results from vibrations, with higher forms of awareness arising out of more complex vibrations. Then, it is no surprise to find that numbers can represent the Universe's vibrations and represent our lives in meaningful, spiritual ways.

There is an energy flow within and between numbers, specifically between the numbers zero and nine. The lower numbers have more significant energy, vibration, and mood changes, but the higher numbers are less contrary.

For example, there are significant differences between the energies of zero and one. In numerology, zero represents the idea of limitlessness and potential, with the concept of being everything, anything, or nothing. On the other hand, one represents the individual focusing on exploration, self-realization, and initiative.

As we advance, later numbers overlap and interlock with each other more seamlessly. For example, the energy of eight leads to integration, institutionalization, and social stability. Eight segues well into nines' energy of humanitarianism, solidarity, compassion, and justice.

As you use the energies of numbers in your life, your goals will realign, or your motivations will transform. Either way, with the aid of recognizing the various energies of numbers, which we will explore in more detail in Chapter 3, you will be able to interpret the destiny better in which the Universe has in store for you.

WHY IS THE FIBONACCI SEQUENCE IMPORTANT?

One example of the patterns that we see in the natural world is the mathematical theorem known as the "Fibonacci Sequence." Linked to the "Golden Ratio," this formula is tied to beauty, creative expression, and symmetry. It is also an example of the ways nature follows numerical patterns.

Leonard Pisano, whose family came from Pisa, Italy, has become famous for his work in mathematics and is often credited with popularizing the Hindu-Arabic system for numerals. While living and working in North Africa, Pisano came to appreciate the simplicity of the ancient number system common to the Middle East. Out of his appreciation for numbers, Pisano, who came to be known as 'Fibonacci,' created a mathematical sequence to describe a phenomenon he had noticed: (a+b)/a = a/b. This sequence results in a numerical pattern that increases in value with each iteration. An example commonly given is "1, 1, 2, 3, 5, 13, 21".

This sequence of numbers is visible within the natural world, from breeding patterns to the shape of seeds and sets of petals on flowers. Although Pythagoras did not formulate the Fibonacci Sequence, he did discuss the "Golden Ratio," which draws on ideas expressed in the Fibonacci Sequence. Both mathematical concepts are visible in human art and architecture, from the Giza Pyramid to Renaissance artists.

Although critics are quick to point out that not all things in nature follow the Fibonacci Sequence or the Golden Ratio, the plethora of examples within nature, which point to mounting 'coincidental' patterns and symmetry, would suggest otherwise. Many numerologists believe that these mathematical equations are examples of the Universe manifesting energy through various numbers.

Pythagoras and Fibonacci were not the only philosophers and mathematicians interested in these patterns. Kabbalah, for example, argues for a world that is structured according to divine numbers. Like Chaldean or Pythagorean numerologists, Kabbalah utilizes numbers to express mystical information hidden and shown throughout life and the Universe. However, Kabbalah has different meanings for their numbers and tie interpretation solely to your name. In contrast, other numerological systems also require birth-dates and other numbers to provide insight into your life fully.

Numerologists, therefore, will use Pythagorean calculations for divining Life Path numbers but may also use calculations linked to names for other significant angel numbers. Based on Kabbalah, some numerical calculations assign a number to each letter of the alphabet.

1	2	3	4	5	6	7	8	9
A	B	C	D	E	F	G	H	I
J	K	L	M	N	O	P	Q	R
S	T	U	V	W	X	Y	Z	

Chapter 6 will provide instructions and interpretations for all forms of numerological calculations, including the Life Path Number, Inner Soul Number, Personality Number, and Birthday Number. With this knowledge and a solid grasp of the variety of numerology available, you will better leverage the energies found within the hidden numbers around you.

WHAT IS THE LAW OF ATTRACTION?

Now that you understand the beauty and symmetry of the Universe, you may feel ready for the next step. It's exciting! But first, we have to clarify a few more things before we study angel numbers. Although our minds may be ready to believe, our souls and hearts must also be prepared to receive this knowledge. Using angel numbers through meditation and prayer to manifest your dreams will only come to fruition when your thoughts, values, and emotions are appropriately adjusted.

The Law of Attraction, simply put, is the idea that "like attracts like." The more you think about something, the more likely it is going to happen. In a sense, change ultimately comes from the inside out. The good news and the bad news is that we can determine the input and output of negativity and positivity in our lives. Since the Universe can read our vibrations, positive or negative, it is essential to cultivate positive thinking.

Therefore, it is crucial to understand how to channel the energy of your life appropriately—and numerology is here to help! Accessing the positivity and optimism found in your angel numbers, you can use the Law of Attraction to increase the benefits of pursuing your destiny.

However, we have to be careful not to cling to harmful beliefs or ideas about ourselves or reality. Misaligned belief systems and our conscious thoughts may also conflict, resulting in destabilized vibrations. For example, when using the Law of Attraction, you will speak positivity and optimism into your life. You might say something like, "I am full of love, and love will come to me." However, if you feel like you don't deserve love deep down, the Law of Attraction will not take hold.

Looking at our previous example, therefore, if you are pursuing love with the Law of Attraction, you will not only speak it out, but you will also visualize this as reality and then live it one day at a time. All of the Laws of the Universe can work in your favor. The Law of Assumption is assuming your wish fulfilled. When doing this, it will come to be. It is critical to believe that what you wish for has already happened. I recommend practicing gratitude around this. Be thankful for something that will be, as if it already was!

WHAT IS MANIFESTATION?

The final step, then, is manifestation. After you calculate and interpret your personal numbers and then draw on their energies and directions to utilize the Law of Attraction, you will be better positioned to manifest your dreams and life goals.

However, it is essential to note that manifestation isn't a set time nor a simple end goal; instead, it is a continuing process that draws you to your destiny. **Manifestation, in short, consists of transformative practices, habits, and attitudes you utilize to change your life and achieve your dreams.** It is a transformation process where your ideas about yourself, your life, your goals, and your world will slowly change as the Universe directs you on the path to a happier, healthier, and more successful you!

What are your goals? What do you really want? What do you need to be healthy and happy? The rat race to get the next best thing is over. Instead of owning you, the material world will be relegated to its rightful place to aid the path to mental health and happiness. You are ready and open to make contact with your spiritual guides and the energies of the Universe and take control of your life. This is the life of manifestation.

WHAT ARE ANGEL NUMBERS?

By now, you may have noticed that I have referred to numbers in numerology as "Angel Numbers." This special expression developed in the early 2000s to describe the numbers that crop up throughout your life, which bring you support and messages from the Universe.

As noted earlier, Pythagorean (and other older numerological systems) track recurring numbers in your daily life as well as within special dates. However, we will learn later in this book, some numerologists and diviners argue that while these numbers always existed within the fabric of reality, spiritual beings are working to bring these numbers to your attention as guidance. **As a result, these particular numbers are often called "Angel Numbers" because Angels are working with these numbers to bring you support and guidance on your path to self-actualization, personal growth, and the achievement of your dreams.**

2

ANGEL NUMBERS

S lowly transforming from the dark of night to a fragile grey-pink, the sky brightens as the sun peeks over the horizon. The world begins to wake up. Perhaps you are just getting a breath of fresh air or going for a jog. In these early hours of dawn, you appreciate the morning songs of birds, the dew on the leaf, and light morning mist. If you take the time to rest against a tree, you may have the chance to soak in all of the beautiful detail and find yourself one step closer in connection to the natural world.

What is so unique is that within the fabric of our natural world—in the symmetry of the snowflake, in the sequencing of petals on a flower, in the spiral of a seashell—the beauty of numbers is hidden in plain sight.

As stated earlier in Chapter 1, **"Angel Numbers" are the numbers, single or multiple-digit, which recur throughout your life or during a specific time.** Angel numbers show themselves through synchronicity, a phenomenon of meaningful recurrences throughout your life. Pythagoras and other numerologists propose that these numbers have always existed within nature or cultures around us. Still, when we need it most, especially if we ask for guidance, numbers will emerge from the cosmic tapestry to give us direction. With the proper study and utilization of these numbers, we can interpret the messages sent to us and recalibrate ourselves and our actions to enrich our lives better.

WHY DO ANGEL NUMBERS OCCUR?

Although I just stated that angel numbers have been occurring since the Universe first came into being, you might wonder why angel numbers appear or disappear. Let's first consider what might be going on behind the scenes of the material world as we know it.

There are many theories and beliefs as to why angel numbers emerge and come to your notice, but nowadays, there are three major theories as to why numerical synchronicities occur.

First, many people believe that God or the cosmos is trying to orient your energies for the good of yourself and the world around you. This theory is tied deeply to the idea that each human on the planet is born for a specific reason, and this destiny can sometimes get lost in the mundane of life. Using angel numbers, Higher Powers are attempting to orient your direction into more empowering paths, positively affecting the world around you.

Second, many numerologists believe that spirits (usually loved ones who have passed) or angel guides/beings are reaching out to help humanity. This theory expresses the power of love found within the Universe's vibrations. It is an encouragement to realize that you are not alone in the world, even if you don't seem to have friends or family to support you right now. These angel or spirit guides draw your attention to synchronicities that already exist to share their love for you and their desire to empower you.

Third, some people look to the soft science of psychology, notably Carl Jung's theory about "the collective unconscious." Simply put, the collective unconscious is something everyone is born with: a collection of ideas and images that humans share throughout time. The unconscious knowledge passed down from your ancestors emerges within dreams, narrative patterns, and fears. Carl Jung also coined the expression 'synchronicity' to describe meaningful or uncanny coincidences which guide our development. It is possible then that those angel numbers come from the collective unconscious as a form of psychological growth.

Therefore, it is essential to reiterate that numerology does not require a specific faith or belief but complements many spiritual frameworks. All of us are walking our unique paths in life. Numerology is simply the call to embrace the energies our guides are happy to share with us.

ARE THE NUMERIC ARRANGEMENTS OF NUMBERS IMPORTANT?

As we note the numerical synchronicities brought to our attention, it is essential to recall that each number holds specific energies and vibrations, particularly the "core numbers": zero through nine. These energies are defined by which single-digit numbers are involved and the order in which they are placed. For example, 'two' in '25' has a different meaning and energy than in 527 or 2020.

When it comes to multiple-digit numbers, particularly with nonrepeating numerical digits (Ex: 527), the placement of numbers is essential. However, numbers with repeating values (Ex: 44 or 555) have extraordinary (often very powerful) meanings. If you notice an emergent pattern of repeating or sequential numbers, such as 2020 or 3456, be encouraged! It is usually a sign that your spirit guides or angels encourage you to continue on the path you are currently pursuing.

In Chapters 4 and 5, we will be looking at multiple-digit numbers in detail. For now, we will cover some of the basics to keep in mind when analyzing multiple-digit numbers.

Reading Three-Digit Numbers—Focus on the Heart

If you receive a recurring three-digit number, the middle number is often considered the heart of the message or the key. Many times, the energies and meanings related to the central number is being emphasized.

Therefore, if your number is 429, the middle number, 'two,' should be your primary focus. Since 'two' is generally interpreted as being related to relationship, communal harmony, optimism, and resilience, the drive of this numerical sequence is an encouragement for you to build a positive relationship with your goal, whether it is a person, a job, or a thing, and move forward with optimism.

BREAK THE NUMBER DOWN

Disregarding the length of the number, it is also vital to break the number down and analyze what each core number means. With higher digit numbers, such as four or five-digit numbers, it is often recommended to read the first three digits and then add the other numbers as specifiers or as emphasis.

For example, if we take the number '6164', we can first analyze 616 and then consider the last number. Another method with larger numbers is to break the number down into three-digit numbers and then combine them. Therefore, 6164 could be first analyzed as '616' and then as '164', with the final interpretation being a melding of the two. As your particular circumstance unfolds, you will know what this number is specifically guiding you to do, which is why meditation and reflection play a large part in manifesting your dreams.

RUN MULTIPLE CALCULATIONS

Another essential step you should not forget is to run multiple calculations on your number. If your number is 6164, you should add the numbers together.

Not only can you add 6 + 1 + 6 + 4 to get 17, but you can then add 1 + 7 to get 8, another hidden number you can take into account. Considering the interpretation above: "We are here to support you as you move forward fearlessly to pursue a new relationship/revitalize your home/take a risk." What other wisdom can we mine with the addition of eight?

'Eight' is linked to personal power, confidence, the manifestation of abundance, success, and world transformation. We could then read the final message as, "Be confident! We, your angels, are here to support you as you move forward fearlessly to pursue a new relationship/renewed home. . . which will empower you for (financial) success!"

Once again, each number for each individual is unique and tailored to their particular life significance. Only you can know what specific goal you have in mind, and only you know what you really need for a healthy, successful life.

HOW DO I RECOGNIZE MY ANGEL NUMBERS?

By now, you might be getting excited to discover and explore your angel numbers! I'm excited for you as well! In this book, we will be covering in detail how to reach out and gain guidance from the Universe and your angel guides. Chapter 6 provides you with clear and practical ways to connect with your angel numbers. For now, I can assure you that your angel numbers are waiting to be discovered. You simply need to ask and then prepare your spirit for openness and awareness. Begin by reaching out to your angels through prayer or other forms of contact (mediums, groups of like-minded people, etc.). Meditation and relaxation techniques, journaling, and other attitudinal and lifestyle choices can better support you on your path of discovery. Later in Chapter 7, I will also focus on specific manifestation techniques that will help you best use your angel numbers to achieve the goals and dreams you have been trying to reach.

Another way to access angel numbers is by uncovering the hidden angel numbers in your life: your birth date and your name.

Calculate Your Life Path and Destiny—and More!

One of the easiest and most straightforward ways to begin engaging with angel numbers is by calculating those already existing in your life. These numbers are hidden in your birth date and your name. The good news is that these calculations are relatively simplistic.

Let's use a randomly generated name, "Pamila Simms," and a randomly generated birthdate, "July 28, 1978", to model our calculations.

Life Path Number: Life Path angel numbers show you your greater purpose. Add the digits which make up the day, month, and year you were born:

(July 28, 1978 = 28-07-1978 = 28071978)

Now, with the date transformed into a long number, we can add all of the digits together and then add the sum as well:

(28071978 = 2+8+0+7+1+9+7+8 = 42 = 4+2 = 6)

Pamila Simms's angel number is 'six.' If the result of your birthdate sum is '11', '22', or '33', don't reduce it any further because these numbers are particularly powerful with solid spiritual significance.

Personal Year Number: Every year in your life holds special promises or challenges for you. To calculate your Personal Year Number, you add your birth month and day to the current year:

(July 28, 2021 = 07-28-2021 = 07282021)
(0+7+2+8+2+0+2+1 = 22 (2+2 =4))

In Pamila's case, her resulting year energies and vibrations are potent and meaningful, being '22'. You can find interpretations for core numbers in Chapter 3, and other unique numbers can be interpreted for yourself using Chapter 4 or other online resources.

Destiny Number: Destiny Numbers show you how you will achieve your goals or express your gifts and talents. As explained in Chapter 1, numerologists assign numbers to letters to gather more information from names.

1	2	3	4	5	6	7	8	9
A	B	C	D	E	F	G	H	I
J	K	L	M	N	O	P	Q	R
S	T	U	V	W	X	Y	Z	

Using this numerological diagram, we can break down a name into more angel numbers. If you have a middle name, be sure to include it as well (Faragher, 2020):

$$\text{Pamila} = (7+1+4+9+3+1 = 25 = 2+5 = 7)$$
$$\text{Simms} = (1 + 9 + 4 + 4 + 1 = 19 = 1+9 = 10 = 1+0 = 1)$$

Your Destiny Number is calculated by adding the final numbers together:

$$(7+1 = 8)$$

In this case, Pamila Simms's Destiny Number is 'eight.'

Soul (Urge) Number: Soul (Urge) Numbers reveal your hidden nature, particularly your desires. Similar to your Destiny Number, Soul angel numbers are calculated using letters, but this time, only the vowels of your name! For Pamila Simms, her vowels would be:

$$Pamila = (a + i + a = 1 + 9 + 1 = 11)$$
$$Simms = i = 9$$

In the case of Pamila Simms, her vowels are easy to differentiate. However, some people may have a 'y' in their name, making things a little complicated. It is recommended that if the 'y' in your name precedes a vowel and creates an additional vowel sound (Nyah), you can count this 'y' as a vowel. If 'y' is the only vowel sound in the syllable (Berry), you can also use this 'y' as a vowel. Otherwise, most 'y' sounds are considered to be consonants.

Pamila Simms's Soul Urge is (9+11), which equals '20'. We can further break down Twenty into 'two' (2+0). However, if her Soul urge was '11', '22', or '33', no further reduction is needed due to the unique spiritual significance of these numbers.

Personality Number: These numbers can reveal your personality characteristics. Usually, you use your full name to calculate this number, but you can also use nicknames to explore other minor features or possibilities. Like Soul

Numbers, Personality Numbers do not use all of the letters in the name, requiring only the consonants:

$$Pamila = (p+m+l = 7+4+3 = 14)$$
$$Simms = (s+m+m+s = 1+4+4+1 = 10)$$

In this case, Pamila Simms's Personality Number is calculated by adding both sums together:

$$(14+10 = 24 = 2+4 = 6)$$

Like the other angel numbers, Personality Number sums that are initially '11', '22', or '33' should not be reduced. Furthermore, if the name begins with a 'y' (Yolanda), the 'y' sound counts as a consonant. Similarly, if the 'y' "follows a vowel in the same syllable and does not provide a separate vowel sound," it is counted as a consonant.

Maturity Number: Maturity Numbers point to an underlying goal in your life that may surface in your mid-30s or 40s, although it will impact most of your life. This goal does not simply define the direction of your life but also expresses the nature of your true or best self. To calculate this you add your Life Path Number and Destiny Number together.

Pamila Simms's Life Path Number is 'six.' Her Destiny Number is 'eight.'

$$(6+8 = 14 = 1+4 = 5)$$

Her Maturity Number, therefore, is 'five.'

We can sum up Pamila Simms's angel numbers as:

- Life Path Number: 6
- Destiny Number: 8
- Soul Urge Number: 2
- Personality Number: 6
- Maturity Number: 5

To read these numbers and understand how they impact your identity, drives, and actions, you can consult Chapter 1 and review the various meanings for each core number. Note them down in your journal and begin the path to connecting with your angel guides through intentional writing and meditation.

WHY ARE MY ANGEL NUMBERS NO LONGER APPEARING TO ME?

What if you have experienced numerical synchronicity before, but they are no longer appearing to you now? Don't worry! There are many explanations as to why angel numbers disappear or change throughout one's lifetime.

In Chapter 6, I will detail the many different reasons why angel numbers may no longer appear to you. It might be because of some personal obstacles you may need to over-come or because your numbers are changing. Or perhaps you have achieved what your angels hoped for you, and you just need to keep going on with the life path in front of you.

Whatever the cause may be, I hope that this book will help and support all readers on their unique life paths. Whether your goals are financial stability, career success, intimate relationships, or personal growth, I aim to equip you better to leverage the energies and vibrations of your angel numbers and manifest the dreams of your heart.

SINGLE-DIGIT ANGEL NUMBERS

> *"The white sun sets beyond the mountains;*
>
> *The Yellow River runs down to the sea.*
>
> *If you want to see further, you must go further up."*

Wang ZhiHuan's famous Tang Dynasty poem, The Ascent, vividly describes a Chinese sunset, but it also holds a subtle reminder for his audience: vision requires perspective. In order to see further, you must ascend the stairs to a higher floor (Wang, 2020). Like Wang ZhiHuan's Chinese tower, numerology offers a fantastic view of your life, but only if you are willing to ascend in your knowledge of angel numbers. They offer a way to gain perspective and provide direction on reaching the goals you place for yourself.

This chapter will be ascending one level in understanding the basic "core numbers" of numerology: zero through nine. With this comprehensive guide, you will be well on your way to interpreting other angel numbers emerging in your daily life. Let's get started!

0

Basic Information:

- Associated Astrological Body: Pluto
- Associated Star Sign: Scorpio
- Associated Tarot: The Fool

The Major Message for You: "Keep doing what you are doing!"

'Zero' represents the totality of the Universe—life, death, and rebirth. It is linked to limitlessness and the pure spirit and is often read as signifying everything, anything, and nothing. Since 'zero' energy is closely tied to the spirit, it usually indicates authenticity and spirituality.

Often, 'zero' in an Angel Number means that your spirit guides or Higher Power is emphasizing something. For example, in an angel number like '50', the 'zero' magnifies the 'five.' It is saying, "Pay close attention to the 'five' energies in your life!". However, when presented singly as a direction, core number zeros are usually meant as an encouragement to keep sticking to the path you are on currently. You are going in the right direction!

1

Basic Information:

- Associated Astrological Body: Sun
- Associated Star Sign: Aries
- Associated Tarot: The Sun/The Magician
- Associated Colors: Red/Yellow
- Associated Letters: A, J, S

The Major Message for You: "Go forward with belief. You will succeed!"

Life Path Number: Unique individualists will need to overcome alienation and loneliness, but they will reach their full potential if they find power in their independence.

Personal Year Number: A year of new beginnings, high energy, and many decisions to make!

Destiny Number: You are self-sufficient and independent. Embrace your uniqueness and help others around you to find their path.

Soul Urge Number: You want to become self-sufficient and independent, hoping to embrace the freedom to be yourself. You want to be a driving force in life and believe sincerely in yourself and your actions as valuable, but you may need to stay humble and attentive.

Personality Number: Courageous, independent, innovative, strong-willed, and creative. Confident, great leaders, and creative, but need to work on their overconfidence, stubbornness, ego, and insensitivity.

Maturity Number: You are moving towards independence and leadership. You will need to either work on being less reliant on others or learn how to depend on others. It would help if you looked for ways to interact with family, friends, and coworkers appropriately and understand how unjust or selfish behavior can injure your relationships and cause negative vibrations, which will impact your ability to manifest.

Career

If number 'one' is emerging concerning your career, your guides may be encouraging you to move forward with a project. You can see it as greenlighting a proposal, a time to take risks, and perhaps, rise to a position of leadership. However, if your Destiny Number is 'one,' the emergence of 'one' in your life should give you cause to reflect on the importance of teamwork within the workplace. As a leader, a destiny charged with the energy of 'one' will need to learn how to harness their abilities appropriately, mainly if their career is characterized by teamwork or team management.

Relationships

Of course, being assertive and independent, people gifted with the number one for their Destiny angel number may struggle to settle down. Ones are in danger of being overly independent, dominant, and aggressive. This results in Ones often expecting too much of a partner or requiring many self-esteem boosts from their partners. When it comes to relationship-building, Ones need to slow down, be patient, and listen. However, when the core number 'one' shows up in your life as a nondestiny number, this may indicate becoming proactive in your relationships. Perhaps taking charge of a directionless trajectory in your life (particularly when it comes to relating to money) will result in unexpected success!

2

Basic Information:

- Associated Astrological Body: Moon
- Associated Tarot: The Moon/The High Priestess
- Associated Colors: Orange/Blue
- Associated Letters: B, K, T

The Major Message for You: "Consider deeply how you are relating to. . ."

Life Path Number: As you work to make the world more harmonious, you must also make sure you will stand with conviction for your ideas and beliefs.

Personal Year Number: A year of building relationships, working with others, and developing emotional connections.

Destiny Number: You have been called to heal and support the people around you, making peace and mediating between people and the world around them.

Soul Urge Number: You want to build a world filled with community and cooperation, where conflicts can be resolved peacefully. You want to be needed, admired, and loved by all. You are motivated to connect deeply with others but struggle to handle conflict and pressure well.

Personality Number: Authentic, compassionate, and non-judgemental, these personalities find the most happiness in helping others. Although they are honest, responsible, reliable, and friendly, Twos need to work on emotional mood swings and social anxiety.

Maturity Number: You are moving towards emotional sensitivity and teamwork. You will need to either work on being less sensitive to people's input or more sensitive, depending on your current personality. While working towards better relationships and teamwork, Twos need to learn how to contribute, shrug off negative input, and receive constructive criticism to boost their ability to contribute to society.

Career

If number 'two' is emerging in relation to your work and career, this may be a call to cooperation or improving your relationship with work. It may also indicate a need to learn how to draw the line and stand up for your ideas and self-expression. The emergence of 'two' may involve increasing sensitivity to others, or conversely, for those with 'two' as a Destiny Number, trust your intuition. One thing to watch out for is competitive or high-stress work environments. As a Two, you may struggle to feel comfortable working in highly debitive workspaces.

Relationships

Of course, being linked to community and companionship, people gifted with 'two' for their Destiny angel number will more easily fall in love, thinking they are ready for a relationship. However, Twos need to be careful not to become swayed by their emotions, sometimes becoming unable to endure difficulties independently. When betrayed, Twos will need to battle fear, bitterness, or jealousy. On the other hand, if 'two' as a core number is showing up in your life, this may be a call for you to embrace or improve relationships, particularly with the person or object of your desire. After all, people are not the only relationships you have in the world! How you relate to money, for example, can be directed by the energy of 'two'.

3

Basic Information:

- Associated Astrological Body: Jupiter
- Associated Star Sign: Gemini
- Associated Colors: Yellow
- Associated Letters: C, L, U

The Major Message for You: "Release what you are holding back!"

Life Path Number: You aren't afraid to express yourself socially and creatively, encouraging others and helping them to connect with themselves.

Personal Year Number: A year of creativity and inspiration for new projects and self-expression.

Destiny Number: You are inspiring and creative, but you need to learn how to focus and organize to achieve your goals.

Soul Urge Number: You have a desire to use your creative talents as a way to support and guide others. You seek pleasure through self-expression and interaction with people, but you may need to work on focus and diligence.

Personality Number: Friendly, independent, and expressive. Threes may struggle with superficiality and frivolousness, but they can grow into supportive, spiritual maturity.

With strong intuition and excellent communication skills, Threes need to be careful of using these abilities to manipulate others.

Maturity Number: You are moving towards creativity and expression. You will need to work on the proper balance of socialization required for you. This means that you may need to either step forward or step back. Pursue an artistic or expressive hobby or skill set that will encourage you to find inner joy and playfulness. You may also be able to use art as a way to better navigate the ups and downs of your emotions.

Career

If you are noticing the angel number 'three,' this is an encouragement to pursue personal freedom and expression in the workplace, perhaps by taking creative risks. It may also mean that you should focus on the present moment or that support and abundance may be coming your way. Maybe it is time to prepare for the opportunity for a raise or promotion coming your way! As a Three, you will be most happy working with other people, as a thespian, human resources manager, or salesperson. However, you may need to learn to persevere because Threes energy may result in a tendency to hop from career to career, resulting in a lot of experience but little skill.

Relationships

As creative expressionists, Threes in romance are active and attractive. They love the passion and romance of a relationship but may struggle with fulfilling their partner's needs on more practical levels. Sometimes, people with intense 'three' energy need to remember that it is as essential to do the dishes as it is to give presents! However, if your Life Path or Destiny Number has no connection to the angel number 'three', and you are noticing a 'three'-pattern, this may be a message of love sent to you from your spirit guides or the Higher Powers. It may also be a warning to pursue personal freedom in your relationships and just be yourself.

Special Note

Since 'three' is linked to spiritual alignment and the idea of spiritual unity (the Trinity), seeing the angel number 'three' in your life might mean that Ascended Masters (or spirit guides) are working to help you manifest your dreams. "Ascended Masters" are great teachers who have achieved wisdom and now work in the spirit realm for your benefit.

4

Basic Information:

- Associated Astrological Body: Uranus
- Associated Star Sign: Taurus
- Associated Tarot: The Emperor
- Associated Colors: Green
- Associated Letters: D, M, V

The Major Message for You: "Take care of the essentials, and with perseverance, you will overcome all odds!"

Life Path Number: Your practicality and responsibility become the foundation others can trust, but you may struggle with feeling trapped or confined.

Personal Year Number: A year of diligence, discipline, and focus which will offer incredible opportunities.

Destiny Number: With hard work and practical organization, you will create something valuable and secure, aiding others around you.

Soul Urge Number: You are independent yet cooperative, hoping to help others around you and bring peace. You want to bring order and beauty into life, but you should not fear the challenges and transformations ahead.

Personality Number: Enthusiastic, productive, and creative, Fours are invested in their family bonds and resist change.

Fours are salt of the earth types who are usually stable, mature, nurturing, and family-oriented, but they may become too serious or lack charisma.

Maturity Number: You are learning how to deal with limitations. You will need to figure out how to focus and organize better to achieve your goals. It may be challenging for you to adopt optimism and organization to work around currently immovable obstacles. Instead of giving into self-defeat and martyrdom, you can learn how to best work with the opportunities you have received to manifest your dreams.

Career

In terms of career and the workplace, if you are noticing the synchronicity of 'four' in your life, it may be a reminder to get back to basics, focus on building firm foundations, and organizing yourself to better manifest your dreams. With an emphasis on harmony and hard work, Four energies are preparing you for a challenge ahead. If the number 'four' is a significant core number, perhaps linked to your Life Path or Destiny Numbers, you will be most successful and fulfilled working with smaller teams or businesses, where loyalty and determination are valued. Sometimes, when you feel overlooked or underappreciated, you may struggle with appropriately voicing your frustrations.

Relationships

If you have 'four' for your Life Path number, you will be a stable, committed, and loyal partner who will focus on caring for and supporting your partner. However, sometimes this nurturing aspect in Fours results in domineering behavior! If you see the number four emerge in your relationships, there are a few meanings to consider. First, know that your guardian angel is watching over you. Second, start applying your organizational and practical skills to your relationships to maximize the relational energies between your partner, family, and friends. Lastly, embrace imperfection in others and allow them to grow at their own pace. With preparation and firm foundations, you and your loved ones will be ready to weather the storms of life together!

Special Note

The number 'four' for many Asian cultures represents bad luck, primarily due to the similarity in sound between the word for 'four' and 'death.' This results in the number four being removed from elevator keypads, apartment numbers, and even phone numbers. For Middle Eastern and European numerologists, the number does not carry such unlucky connotations. However, it is interesting to note that 'four' is a dividend of eight, often linked to challenge and difficulty in numerology. Therefore, if 'four' does emerge as a pattern in your life, it may not be necessarily saying that you are doomed; rather, it may be a call to perseverance and diligence to overcome difficulty ahead.

5

Basic Information:

- Associated Astrological Body: Jupiter
- Associated Star Sign: Leo
- Associated Tarot: The Hierophant
- Associated Colors: Blue
- Associated Letters: E, N, W

The Major Message for You: "Time for a transformation!"

Life Path Number: You thrive within environments of activity and transformation; however, you may struggle with building healthy routines for yourself.

Personal Year Number: A year of transformation, change, and freedom to explore yourself, life, and new opportunities for development.

Destiny Number: Your sense of adventure, together with your intelligence and curiosity, will bring you many experiences and will allow you to help others to embrace change.

Soul Urge Number: You need variety and freedom in your life, preferring to change things up. However, remember that building firm foundations are necessary, too! You want to learn about everything, but you need to work on being committed and stable for your relationships.

Personality Number: Individualistic, positive, and adaptable. Fives pursue personal freedom and adventure, but they need to be careful not to give into impulsivity and indulgence. Since they are up for everything and are highly adaptable, Fives can sometimes take on too much.

Maturity Number: You are moving towards transformation and freedom. You have been given the liberty to embrace change and learn new things. This doesn't mean that you should spiral into excessive behaviors (related to food, substances, or sex), but rather utilize this energy to evaluate your habits and approaches to reaching your goals. With a new perspective from this number's energies, you may achieve manifestation in ways before you hadn't considered.

Career

For those noticing an angel number 'five' emerging regarding career or work, this may be a sign to change things up. The number 'five' is a sign that you shouldn't be afraid of the future opportunity to transform. Those who have a Life Path or Destiny Number linked to Fives energies should remember that their desire for adventure and freedom may interfere with their ability to deal with conflict or monotony appropriately. Fives should pursue careers that involve travel, change, or high interaction with people, which promotes intellectual and spiritual stimulus. Also, Fives need to remember to see quietness and routine as a chance to focus and grow in skill and knowledge.

Relationships

With this intense focus on freedom to explore the physical or spiritual worlds, Fives need a lot of room to thrive. As for Fives themselves, they need to learn that running away from "boring stuff" or uncomfortable conflict in relationships will ultimately undermine their happiness. On the other hand, if you see a pattern of Fives emerging in your life regarding love or relationships, this may be a call to change things up or be open for a new opportunity to find love again. Perhaps it is time to reassess the status of your current relationship and make sure that you are not being caught up in a toxic partnership. For others, since the pattern of 'fives' reveals itself in the human body (the five senses, etc.), it may be a call to reorient your body to manifest your goals and self-expression better.

6

Basic Information:

- Associated Astrological Body: Venus
- Associated Star Sign: Virgo
- Associated Tarot: The Lovers

- Associated Colors: Indigo/Purple and Green
- Associated Letters: F, O, X

The Major Message for You: "Time to reassess how you are spending your time and energy!"

Life Path Number: You love to support, help, and care for others, but you also need to remember to take care of yourself!

Personal Year Number: A year of serving people, dealing with family or home affairs, and getting work done.

Destiny Number: As you work to make the world a better place, you will discover a world of beauty and creativity, but you also need to work on self-care.

Soul Urge Number: You want to build a world of love and harmony, which can sometimes end up with too much self-sacrifice on your part. You want to care for others and work to make the world a better place, but be careful that you remain optimistic and open-hearted, whatever the consequences.

Personality Number: Dependable, loving, and generous. You are the rock everyone depends on, but you can also become bossy, a perfectionist, and anxious. Though warm-hearted, responsible people, Sixes will need to watch out for anxiety, impulsive spending, and oversensitivity.

Maturity Number: You are moving towards building a community and serving it. As you access the energies of 'six' for maturity, you will learn how to handle and balance responsibilities better. You will be able to counsel others and be more involved with your family, but you will also need to make sure that you don't end up turning into a self-righteous busybody! With the stability and balance of 'six,' you will slowly but surely achieve manifestation.

Career

Seeing synchronicity in your life linked to the energies of angel number 'six' is a warning sign to consider how you are investing your time and energy, particularly when it comes to balancing work and personal life, as well as material and spiritual needs. It may be a call to serve others, but at the same time, it may also be a reminder to provide support thoughtfully, not forgetting to prioritize your own needs and identity. For those who identify as a Six for their Life Path or Destiny Number, you may find the cutthroat atmosphere of some careers off-putting, preferring to work in team-oriented spaces, such as teaching, diplomacy, or art. Sensitive to the needs of others, you may struggle to say 'no,' and as a result, undermine your own mental health and personal stability.

Relationships

As supportive, caring individuals, Sixes are attractive partners, but often for the wrong reasons, and they may end up settling with an emotionally or financially predatory person. Although Sixes are perfect for building a family, their loving characteristics may make it hard for them to stand up for themselves during a conflict, resulting in unhealthy compromises. If you see the angel number 'six' emerge in terms of your relationships, you should see this as a sign to pursue and tend to the personal relationships in your life. 'Six' is usually a sign for you to reassess any imbalances in your life that may be separating you from your loved ones and their support.

7

Basic Information:

- Associated Astrological Body: Saturn
- Associated Star Sign: Libra
- Associated Tarot: The Chariot
- Associated Colors: Violet/Purple and Grey
  Associated
- Letters: G, P, Y

The Major Message for You: "Take this moment to align with Divine Purpose."

Life Path Number: Driven to pursue spiritual enlightenment and psychic alignment with Higher Powers. You seek knowledge, contemplation, and beauty and must reject pessimism and pride.

Personal Year Number: A year of introspection, spiritual development, and increased self-awareness may lead to spiritual awakening.

Destiny Number: You are always searching for philosophical, spiritual, and psychological truth for yourself and others. Be careful of pride and passivity!

Soul Urge Number: Your drive to understand yourself and the Universe around you is born from a need to understand the truth and may result in pride and depression. You want to find meaning in the Universe and question everything, but make sure that you trust in your truth and keep connected to humanity.

Personality Number: Spiritual, analytical, and questioning. Sevens seek a higher purpose but can become intolerant, cynical, and isolated. Sevens can struggle to connect well with people emotionally and socially, but they hold great wisdom and incredibly rational perspectives to help people in their lives.

Maturity Number: You are moving towards spiritual maturity found in meditation and meaningful spiritual practices. This growth may involve you having to isolate yourself for a time to retreat from the world's pressures to find your truths. As a result, you may learn more about your spiritual self and work towards psychological and intellectual break-throughs. During this process, make sure that you don't leave friends and family high and dry. Be sure to let them know what is going on in your life!

Career

Angel number 'seven' appearing in your life is usually a sign that your guides are pleased with your progress. New opportunities may be opening up ahead, especially opportunities to grow spiritually, even during difficult times. It could also mean that it's time to take a break from work and go on a holiday to reorient your spirit and boost your vibrations to prepare for further spiritual awakening. If your Life Path or Destiny Number is a 'seven,' you will benefit from intellectually and spiritually stimulating jobs, such as being a doctor. Sevens, however, are not simply satisfied with money or career advancement. Their spiritual health matters as well, so taking time to volunteer or travel is just as important. Also, Sevens should be sure to choose a career or workplace that aligns with their spiritual and ethical value system.

Relationships

In love, Sevens are very romantic, often moving quickly through the stages of love. This fast pace may not always work with their partners, so Sevens must be patient and self-aware to not mistaken infatuation for long-term romance. Being more creative, intellectual, and spiritual, Sevens benefit from having a more practical, "down-to-earth" partner who can help them focus and stay organized in their pursuits. When seeing the angel number 'seven' appear in conjunction with relationships, this may be a call to practice some self-love and introspection, taking time out to relax and regain some independence. 'Seven' also reminds us that our spirit guides, angels, and Higher Powers love us and are happy with the progress we have made in our lives.

8

Basic Information:

- Associated Astrological Body: Saturn/North Node of the Moon
- Associated Star Sign: Leo
- Associated Tarot: Strength
- Associated Colors: Silver
- Associated Letters: H, Q, Z

The Major Message for You: "You are an overcomer! You've got this!"

Life Path Number: You rise above adversity and obstacles to achieve your dreams, most often connected with material success. Just make sure that your obsessive, workaholic nature does not erode your spiritual health and personal relationships.

Personal Year Number: A year of abundance and reward, including material possessions, wealth, or recognition.

Destiny Number: Finding fulfillment in leading others, you are driven by money, power, and success but will need to learn how to balance your work and personal life.

Soul Urge Number: You are ambitious, pursuing financial and career success as the path to happiness. However, you need to make sure that your authoritative nature doesn't drive others away or trample on them. You want to secure power and status and work hard for it, but you need to make sure that you don't get swallowed up by the material world at the expense of your spiritual health.

Personality Number: Optimistic, extraverted, and confident, Eights attract others with their power and charisma but need to curb their greedy and domineering behavior. Successful, intuitive, and self-controlled, Eights will get very far, but they do need to work on their authoritarian, boastful sides.

Maturity Number: You are moving onto a mature attitude towards reward and accomplishment. Not only do you understand that reward follows hard work and organization, but also you understand the importance of accepting and healthily embracing abundance. Instead of being consumed by wealth, possessions, and status, you know their proper place in your life as you pursue manifestation and healthy relationships with others around you.

Career

The appearance of 'eight' in your life is usually a warning sign that obstacles or adversity are looming soon. Embracing positivity and ambition, this is a challenge for you to overcome with the promise of a long-term spiritual and psychological payoff. In terms of career, this may mean that there are roadblocks ahead, but you will be in a better position to manifest your life goals if you overcome them. Those with 'eight' in their Life Path or Destiny Number will have the drive to succeed. With excellent organizational and practical skills, Eights know how to manage people and other variables at work. Eights can use their leadership skills to better society, particularly for humanitarian enterprises in a healthy mental and spiritual state. Something Eights need to be careful of is taking on all of the responsibility or glory for their own.

Relationships

Interestingly, Eights (in the realm of relationships) are at their most vulnerable. As a result, they may be reluctant to share their emotions with loved ones, resulting in rocky relationships early in life. However, with maturity, Eights may learn how to better partner with a loved one, providing support and energy. If you see 'eight' emerge as a pattern in your life, it may be a call to take leadership in a particular relationship. Instead of feeling like you don't deserve wealth or happiness, the energy of the angel number 'eight' is a reminder that you can overcome all obstacles in your relationships and receive abundance with the attitude of positivity and ownership. Remember that relationships don't just mean connecting with people, but also your ideas and associations with money or advancement.

Special Note

In Buddhism, Karma is linked to the Noble Eightfold Path, which numerologists refer to as the "Universal Spiritual Law of Cause and Effect." As such, 'eight' is a Karmic Number indicating "that the time for karma in this life has come." Depending on your Karma from your past life or actions, this may forewarn of negative or positive events that are coming. However, this should not be a cause for alarm. If positive Karma is coming your way, 'eight' reminds you to welcome it with open arms. If negative Karma is coming your way, 'eight' reminds you to weather the storm and emerge even stronger and better!

9

Basic Information:

- Associated Astrological Body: Uranus/South Node of the Moon
- Associated Star Sign: Sagittarius
- Associated Tarot: The Hermit
- Associated Colors: Gold
- Associated Letters: I, R

The Major Message for You: "Love yourself! Love others!"

Life Path Number: Your compassion and generosity drive you to make the world a better place, but you also need to understand that imperfection is a fact of life.

Personal Year Number: A year of completion and celebration, offering the potential beginning of a new phase and transformation.

Destiny Number: You must forgive yourself and overcome prejudice and judgemental feelings towards others to fulfill your destiny, transforming the world around you into a more compassionate, beautiful place.

Soul Urge Number: You want to promote peace, unity, and forgiveness through charitable work and supporting the people in your life. You want to make the world a better place and pursue humanitarian work to that end, but make sure that you don't end up prideful or pushy when guiding others.

Personality Number: Charismatic, compassionate, and invested, Nines are often the center of attention. They may struggle with lethargy, disconnection, and insensitivity. Philanthropic Nines are influential, charismatic, and confident, but sometimes they will come off as entitled, cocky, or aloof.

Maturity Number: You are moving towards generosity and self-sacrifice that is almost transcendental. Letting go of yourself, you embrace the divine purpose of the Universe and work to improve the world around you. You will find the most happiness in counseling, healing, or teaching others, particularly regarding spiritual health. Abandoning selfishness, indifference, and mercilessness, you will make the world a better place and achieve manifestation.

Career

During times of difficulty or conflict at work, the emergence of 'nine' is seen as solid encouragement from your angel guides that you are not alone. Since 'nine' is three multiplied three times, the energy of nine is often linked to the idea of renewal, completion, and ascension. Nine energies also direct you to exercise compassion and tolerance in the service of others around you. As a Nine, you will enjoy the challenge of deadlines and appropriate pressure at your job. Nines enjoy change and challenge, mainly when linked to helping improve society, such as teaching, police work, soldiery, and environmentalism. Hard-working, driven Nines will need to remember to be patient with others who need calmer or slower work environments.

Relationships

As stated previously, Nines have innate compassion and generosity of spirit, which makes them attractive partners. In love with the idea of love, Nines are affectionate partners who enjoy the passion and excitement of romance and relationships. However, Nines need to learn how to moderate their jealousy and tantrums when dealing with disappointments in their partnerships. With time and maturity, Nines become committed, protective partners and friends who are also aware of their own needs and leave toxic relationships when required. If you see 'nine' pop up in your life, particularly in terms of your friendships, family, and romantic relationships, this is a sign to redirect your energies toward building better connections with a focus on compassion, forgiveness, and kindness. It is a call to listen to your partner and consider their needs and desires. With the energy of nine, your relationships will move towards mutual respect and understanding.

BUILDING THE FOUNDATION

Core numbers are the building blocks of numerological interpretation, providing you with a unique number that may define your Life Path, Destiny, or Soul Urge Number. These numbers will give specific energies or vibrations within larger numbers as well.

Pan, in her article, "Numerology Basics: The Ultimate Beginner's Guide" (2020), sums up the core numbers as follows:

1. Individuality, independence, initiative, determination, selfishness
2. Sensitivity, compromise, harmony, balance, overly compliant
3. Creativity, enthusiasm, optimism, inspiration, superficial
4. Stability, tradition, hard work, security, unchangeable
5. Change, freedom, progressiveness, sensuality, unstable
6. Care, responsibility, family, romanticism, conventional
7. Loneliness, mysticism, skepticism, enlightenment, perfectionism
8. Power, success, abundance, influence, domination
9. Forgiveness, compassion, community, reward, lethargy

Now that you understand the power and energy of each core number, you are better equipped to move towards manifesting your dreams and goals. Your journey to self-fulfillment and success is well underway!

REPEATING ANGEL NUMBERS

You probably have experienced this before—blearily jolting awake at the insistent 'beep-beep' of your alarm clock. Maybe you roll over and try to ignore it. Perhaps you hit the snooze button for another five minutes of peace. Maybe you sit up in a half-slump and sigh. It's too early in the morning for you. Why did you want to get up again?

Then, your alarm sounds again. It's that annoying but so necessary wake-up call you need. At the end of a long day, you set the alarm again, knowing that achieving everything you want to get done will require getting up on time.

Just like an alarm bell or a siren, repeating angel numbers can be seen as a strong call from your angels or spirit guides. Numbers like 999 or 55 are particularly powerful messages from the Universe to connect to a unique vibration because they continue multiplied energies of a specific core number. Many repeating numbers should be interpreted as encouragement, guidance, reminders, promises, or warnings.

Let's have a look at the special meanings of repeating double, triple, and quadruple-digit number patterns.

REPEATING ZEROS

00

A Major Message for You: You have the freedom to choose your path.

If this number begins to recur in your life, it means that you are in a phase where you are free to make choices about your life. It is a time for great potential and power, so you must remain calm and sensitive to the directions of the Universe. At this time, you should practice faith and embrace adventure moving forward, yet also make sure to analyze your options carefully and wisely. If faced with a challenge too great for you to overcome, this may be reassurance from your angel guides to change direction as necessary. Have faith in yourself and your abilities. Your journey has just begun!

What Your Future Holds: A whole new vista is opening up for you.

What You Can Do:

- Stay calm.
- Analyze your options.
- Step forward in faith.

000

A Major Message for You: Angels are here to guide you!

The appearance of '000' in your life brings encouragement with the knowledge that your angel guides or Higher Power is with you, watching over and loving you. They are ready to connect with you and work in your life, bringing you to a greater realization of the part you have to play in this cosmic story. Stay strong and have faith in the talents and gifts that you have been given. The challenges you face will pass. You are one with God, and He loves you.

What Your Future Holds: Challenges you may be facing now, or very soon, will pass.

What You Can Do:

- Connect with your spiritual guides through meditation and prayer.
- Affirm through manifestation the Universe's love for you.
- Weigh your options carefully.

A Major Message for You: The potential for positive change is ripening.

Although potentially a number with connections to bad luck and difficulty, '0000' can be seen as an opportunity to challenge yourself and change for the better. Linked to both the end-times and endlessness, you are faced with the binary reality accompanying all choices. As a result, it is essential to determine the nature of your transformation and path going forward by manifesting positivity. It is a time to attract and initiate a new future, but make sure it is the future you want! Now is the time for you to redirect your Karma by learning from your past, asking for forgiveness, and moving on from toxic habits and relationships.

0000

What Your Future Holds: A choice to pursue a new path with new challenges.

What You Can Do:

- Assess your intentions and determine where you want to invest your energies.
- Ask for forgiveness—redirect your Karma.
- Focus on positivity and change.
- Move on from toxic relationships.

REPEATING ONES

11

A Major Message for You: Get ready for spiritual change.

With the emergence of '11' in your life, this is a sure sign that an opportunity for spiritual enlightenment or awakening has arrived. It's time for you to learn about yourself, the Universe, and your place in it. Don't be afraid to seek the truth, even if it means that some of your beliefs or ideas will change. The result will be not only stronger spiritual connections but also positive output into the world. As you start fresh, you will feel the call to lead people to a better life, focusing on harmony and healing, which is sometimes called 'lightwork.' Since '11' is linked to 2 (1+1=2) holds encouragement to pursue harmony and healing. Get ready to start this new path in life by letting go of addictions and distractions but rather affirming life-changing positive choices.

What Your Future Holds: Opportunities to refresh one's spiritual life as well as change your creative or work-related outlets.

What You Can Do:

- Schedule to break bad habits.
- Minimize social media and other distractions.
- Start a new hobby or job and embrace creativity.

111

A Major Message for You: Monitor your thoughts, as the Universe is listening.

'111' promises a new start, where you can leave the past behind you to move forward to a better future. However, you cannot just take hold of these new opportunities. You must also make sure your thoughts and emotions are aligned correctly with your life purpose. The Universe can read your conscious and unconscious negativity, which can affect the outcome of this energy. Maintaining positivity, therefore, is vital, as well as exploring your inner self and properly communicating with your angel guides. At this time, your powers for manifestation are increased. The reason is that '111' has a hidden link to three (1+1+1 =3), which has ties to spiritual awakening and creative power. Don't overthink it, though! Use the creative energy of '111' to serve others and awaken yourself.

What Your Future Holds: A chance to manifest your desires and dreams.

What You Can Do:

- Serve others through volunteer work.
- Use journaling to monitor your thoughts.
- Reach out to your spirit guides for direction.

1111

A Major Message for You: You can achieve it all!

With the lucky number '1111', you need to recognize this as a compelling wake-up call to manifest your dreams. You can achieve this by faith in yourself, positive thinking, and hard work. Linked to four (1+1+1+1 = 4), the energies of '1111' also remind you that you are loved and watched over by your spirit guides. It also means that it is time to work on your personal and spiritual development by reading and studying meaningful scriptures while doing manifestation work. It is necessary to stress how crucial your actions are at this point, as your angels are encouraging you to take action, work hard, pursue intentional thinking, and discover yourself. A fresh perspective and self-confidence will guide you in the next steps of your life path.

What Your Future Holds: Good luck and abundance are up ahead.

What You Can Do:

- Take note of your dreams and analyze them for important messages.
- Listen for any words from deceased loved ones.
- Reprioritize the material world by minimizing your belongings and analyzing what you really need vs. what you want.

- Speak and write intentional, powerful messages to yourself.

REPEATING TWOS

22

A Major Message for You: Make your dream of a harmonious, loving world a reality.

The revelation of '22' in your life is a call to work on your soul's purpose, which in this case, may involve creating a world of harmony, love, and kindness. Of course, this will require work and organization. Since 2+2=4, '22' has strong links to the diligence and practicality of angel number four's energies. It is not just about feeling good, but also about making practical differences in your own life and others. Sometimes, the appearance of '22' indicates a coming change in the domestic or romantic sphere—new love or a new baby! As you serve others, however, don't forget to focus on your own needs and potential. This is as much a time about loving yourself as it is about loving others. In the process of personal and spiritual growth, you will find yourself more able to help others who are struggling with finding out their purpose in life. Now is the time to make dreams come true.

What Your Future Holds: Changes in the romantic or familial sphere. New partnerships.

What You Can Do:

- Take care of yourself and set aside me-time.
- Listen carefully to the struggles that your family, friends, or coworkers are experiencing.
- Work with numerology to focus on your current soul purpose.

222

A Major Message for You: Trust in yourself and in the goodness of the Universe.

Sometimes, when your life feels chaotic, it is essential to feel a sense of peace. '222' is an encouragement to remember that your intuition and spiritual guidance will not lead you astray. The energy of '222' helps you to control your fears and emotions as you pursue harmony and balance. At this time, unwind and be in the moment, especially as you move forward with projects or work through obstacles that arise. Furthermore, '222' may also bring to your attention old challenges you had failed at prior. With the growth, you have experienced and strong support networks, you will overcome past failures this time around. Linked to Number 6 (2+2+2=6), '222' draws on six's energies, encouraging healthier family connections and work-life balance. Chapter 7 will learn how to use the "222 Manifestation Technique", which uses this particularly powerful angel number for supportive purposes.

What Your Future Holds: Potential challenges.

What You Can Do:

- Meditate or practice yoga for increased mindfulness.
- Rework your schedule to maintain a better balance of work and rest.
- Speak and write positivity into your life with meaningful, intentional sentences.
- Get in touch with family or deceased loved ones for support.

2222

A Major Message for You: Find peace in absolute faith.

If '2222' shows up in your life, this is a call to balance between home and work life as the path to spiritual growth and success. Without harmony and order, peace and tranquility will not blossom. As a result, you need to trust everything will be OK and focus on taking care of yourself. As you visualize your dreams fully and intentionally, you will be better poised to embrace the abundance coming your way. Since '2222' is linked to eight (2+2+2+2=8), the action-oriented energies of 'eight' are vital in this message, suggesting that now is the time to let manifestation take over. Live in the moment and learn to relax as well. When you place absolute faith in your spirit guides or Higher Powers, you will be able to embrace the will of the Universe and grow in love and acceptance. '2222' is your angels' gentle reminder to be courageous and trust in the plan for your life.

What Your Future Holds: A challenge that allows you to grow in faith and confidence.

What You Can Do:

- Take time off for a spa trip, staycation, or mini-vacation.
- Practice yoga to increase mindfulness and relaxation.
- Visualize, fully, the things and people you want to see in your life.

REPEATING THREES

33

A Major Message for You: Your selfless acts of service will elevate your spirit.

The Number 3 traditionally holds a lot of spiritual meaning with connections to the 'Trinity' in Christianity and the "Third Eye" in Buddhism. '33' is a strong call on the part of your angel guides to reconnect your physical life with the spiritual. With the emergence of '33', you are encouraged to reach out and help someone else. This may end up being part of your journey to understanding your spiritual purpose. Since '33' often appears during times of crisis, its energies draw you to positive thinking and working towards change. At this time, you should pursue manifestation techniques. Since '33' is linked to six (3+3=6), '33's' energies connect creativity and self-sacrificing love as a way to serve those around you. During these periods, you are ready for spiritual enlightenment as you utilize imagination and creativity to pursue your dreams, teach yourself lessons, and focus on your priorities. Don't hold yourself back.

What Your Future Holds: A chance to connect with Ascended Masters while negotiating difficulty in life.

What You Can Do:

- Serve others through volunteer work.
- Cut off depressive and negative thinking and speak words of positivity aloud.
- Read past journal entries to understand how you have grown.
- Improve communication skills through mindful speech.

333

A Major Message for You: You are aligned with your angels.

Receiving '333' as an angel message is a cause for confidence and peace. It means that you are aligned with your angels, and you will reach your goals. You can be confident in your abilities and explore all possibilities open for you. Since '333' is linked to nine (3+3+3=9), this number contains similar vibrations, which promote spiritual growth and completion, as well as opportunities to heal the world around you (known as 'lightwork'). With the amplified creative energies of three, you will be able to increase manifestation. At this point in time, it is essential to maintain control and communicate clearly with those around you and contact your spirit guides. '333' may also be pointing to an opportunity to learn from an Ascended Master (like the Virgin Mary or Quan Yin) who has come near to you. As you talk with your Ascended Master, your heart must be open for any wisdom they share. Take this moment to recognize your life purpose and utilize your talents correctly. As you are true to yourself and your desires, you will be better positioned to manifest long-term success. It is essential to listen to your truth at this time and not allow yourself to become derailed by negative opinions or advice from other people around you.

What Your Future Holds: Opportunity to study under an Ascended Master.

What You Can Do:

- Study spiritual materials—prayers, meditations, scriptures, and songs.
- Meditate and pray.
- Participate in lightwork through verbal and practical support of grieving for wounded people around you.

3333

A Major Message for You: Practice visualization to manifest your dreams.

Holding great amplification of the Number 3, '3333's' energy enables maximum creative energy and inspiration for work and artistic expression. '3333' encourages and supports you as you visualize so that you can achieve manifestation more quickly. As we form our desires under this number, we will generate passion which promotes positivity and success. More than just material possession, '3333' heralds meaningful, spiritual experiences that will increase your bond with the Universe. Since 'three' is tied to the "3-6-9 Principle" and links back to itself (3+3+3+3 = 12 = 1+2 = 3), it is a powerful manifestation number linked to creativity and spiritual expression. When communicating with your angels, this number encourages you to ask for clarification, particularly when options seem overwhelming. At this time, it is excellent to know that your angels and Ascended Masters are there to help you be the best you can be as a person. As you manifest positivity and seek inspiration, you will find opportunities to build social connections and inspire others.

What Your Future Holds: Opportunities for creativity and artistic expression.

What You Can Do:

- Visualize, fully, the end product of your projects and dreams.
- Keep your daydreams positive.
- Network thoughtfully.
- Be tolerant and compassionate towards friends, family, and coworkers.

REPEATING FOURS

44

A Major Message for You: You are loved.

When your difficulties feel overwhelming, you may notice '44' appear as a word of encouragement from your angel guides, telling you that you are loved. The energy found in '44' reminds you to keep working throughout the storm because you will fulfill your wishes in time. Trusting your instincts becomes the key to eventual success. You must be patient, diligent, and persevering since circumstances may feel overwhelming and make you doubt your choices. Be reassured, as '44' is positive encouragement to keep fighting. During this period of your life, your angels want you to know that they are still there. They are working as hard as you are on the abundance that is coming. Forthcoming abundance is found within '44's' link to eight (4+4=8). As a result, channel eight's energies of action, confidence, and passion for achieving a positive future. Let go of unnecessary fear—you've got this!

What Your Future Holds: Abundance and success.

What You Can Do:

- Stay on track with well-paced scheduling.
- Pursue positive life choices and habits on a day-to-day basis.
- Visualize, fully, the things and people you want to see in your life.
- Don't focus on your past mistakes; instead, focus on your past achievements.

444

A Major Message for You: Time to leverage your gifts and talents.

If '444' is making an appearance in your life, this is a call to spiritual awakening and an opportunity for manifestation. Use the gifts you have been given, as you have received encouragement to keep going and work hard to overcome the obstacles you may be facing. The good news is that you are not alone, for your angels are working alongside you. Don't lose sight of your soul's mission because you are so close to the top. Linked to the energies of three (4+4+4= 12 = 1+2 = 3), '444' points to the need for spiritual and personal communication (as well as creativity) as a means to achieving your goals. With the amplification of four's energies, '444' reminds us to keep working hard and set firm foundations for future success. '444' also tells you that you are on the right path, although you may not feel like it. During these periods, you should pursue spiritual study and renewed awareness. Don't give up. Your aspirations are almost achieved.

What Your Future Holds: Spiritual awakening or manifestation of your dreams.

What You Can Do:

- Practice meditation to increase mindfulness and focus.
- Find ways to block out distractions, such as muting your phone.
- Connect and communicate with your spirit guides for wisdom and encouragement.
- Study spiritual materials—prayers, meditations, scriptures, and songs.

4444

A Major Message for You: Make your dreams come true.

When '4444' appears as a pattern in your life, see it as a massive cheerleading shout from your angels. Put every effort into your work, and success will come! Of course, you should take your time to accomplish everything well, but you will be unbeatable if you get rid of negativity in your life. With organization and time management, your path will become clear, and results will begin to appear. Therefore, you can see '4444' as signaling a time to celebrate and relax a little. It's important, after all, to find a balance between work and rest. Linked to seven (4+4+4+4= 16 = 1+6 =7), '4444' holds additional encouragement to pursue self-improvement and development. As you work, you are called to listen to your spirit guides and do what is right for you. Right now, times might feel difficult, but change is right around the corner. With support from your angels, you can know that your hard work, focus, and strength will not go unrewarded. Positivity will manifest the desirable changes you seek, which will help you to support and encourage others.

What Your Future Holds: Manifestation.

What You Can Do:

- Stay focused and on track with well-paced scheduling and optimized workspaces.
- Mute social media to minimize distractions and negativity.
- Find time to relax a little—nature walks or meditation sessions.
- Celebrate ahead of time!

REPEATING FIVES

55

A Major Message for You: Take care of yourself.

If you are seeing the '55' angel number pattern, this is the time to pause and look after yourself. Since five's energies promise change and potential challenges, it is essential to take care of yourself and pursue balance in your life. Not only should you try to eat healthy foods, drink lots of water, and get plenty of sleep, but you should also take this opportunity to undergo spiritual cleansing. Let go of negative past experiences, forgive those who have wronged you, and bury old grudges that are distracting you. Five's energies represent change, but not all change is good, so you need to take this moment to prepare yourself for whatever challenges or opportunities are coming your way. Without physical and spiritual balance, the transitions of five's energy may cause you to spiral out of control. Drawing on the power of one (5+5=10 = 1+0 = 1), '55' is telling you, "Don't be afraid! Put your best foot forward, and your life may never be the same!"

What Your Future Holds: Positive or negative change and challenges.

What You Can Do:

- Hydrate and eat well.
- Be sure to get a full eight hours of sleep.
- Through journaling and other forms of therapy, process grudges.

555

A Major Message for You: Great change is coming. Make it happen!

Change is coming! Like all 'five' angel numbers, '555' amplifies a message about oncoming transformations through challenge and change, both positive and negative. At this time, it is important to stay positive as you transition. Trust yourself and your angels as you overcome obstacles to personal growth. It is a time of affirmative change, so taking care of your emotional, mental, and spiritual well-being is key. The good news is that this change may happen over time in small increments. Either way, '555' is a warning to prepare so that you can make the best of this extremely energetic time to harness the powers of transformative vibrations. With connection to six's energies (5+5+5=15 = 1+5=6), '555' also reminds us that the best way to keep balanced and maintain perspective is to connect with the Universe. As you let go of negativity, both past, and present, you can better access the visions that your angels are ready to share with you. Chapter 7 will learn how to use the "555

Manifestation Technique", which uses this mighty angel number for transformative purposes.

What Your Future Holds: Major change is coming.

What You Can Do:

- Pursue positive life choices and habits on a day-to-day basis.
- Meditate or practice yoga for increased mindfulness.
- Rework your schedule to maintain a better balance of work and rest.
- Speak and write positivity into your life with meaningful, intentional sentences.

5555

A Major Message for You: There's no time to be distracted.

'5555' is a call from your angels to stay focused. It is not the time to get depressed or distracted because significant change is around the corner, bringing you new chances to grow and achieve manifestation. Don't be afraid, as your angels are with you and help guide you to know where and when to use your energy. '5555' carries the energies of decision-making and life changes, but we need to make sure that our choices are healthy and strategic to aid us in the process of manifestation. During this time, you might feel anxious, but it is important to remain optimistic. With the power of '5555', your angels are encouraging you to blossom into new levels of faith and strength of character. Focus on your internal truths, ignoring external validations, depressive talk, or past fears. '5555' draws on the energies of two as well (5+5+5+5= 20 = 2+0= 2), which carries encouragement. You are not alone. Your angels are here to help you every step of the way. With this reassurance, stand firm with optimism to manifest the bright future you have claimed for yourself already.

What Your Future Holds: Opportunities to take charge of your life.

What You Can Do:

- Stay focused and on track with well-paced scheduling and optimized workspaces.
- Mute social media to minimize distractions and negativity.
- Find a supportive friend to strategize with and get new perspectives.
- Pursue intentional speech and visualizations to direct your energies better.

REPEATING SIXES

66

A Major Message for You: Heal your soul, and heal others.

The number '66' may appear in your life when times are challenging or overwhelming. '66', linked to the angel number three (6+6=12 = 1+2= 3), is a reminder that you are not alone, as your angels are close by and are working on ways to help you achieve manifestation. The presence of 'three' also points to a need to embrace creativity and communication to achieve balance in your life. You may need to work on many areas—the balance between work and home life or even the balance between family and personal life. Find time to nurture others, but also remember to take care of yourself as well! Prioritize physical and spiritual health by pursuing fitness or working on past trauma. As balance and stability in relationships and work are restored, you will be better positioned to engage with your motherly energies to nurture others. '66' tells you that love and compassion for yourself are just as important as it is for other people.

What Your Future Holds: A better day, a better you.

What You Can Do:

- Serve others through volunteer work.
- Pursue positive life choices and habits on a day-to-day basis.
- Through journaling and other forms of therapy, process grudges, and traumas.
- Rework your schedule to fit in time for self-care and family life.

666

A Major Message for You: Align yourself with Truth and the Universe.

For Christians, '666' is related to evil, but in numerology, it is linked to the positive energies of nine (6+6+6= 18 = 1+8 = 9), which represents the energies of spiritual completion and healing. Therefore, seeing '666' emerging as a pattern in your life may point to an opportunity to align with transformative spiritual powers. This number may appear during times of challenge to help you stay positive, get back on track, and achieve your dreams, despite the circumstances. Through meditation, introspection, and healing interaction with angel guides and family, you must pursue a balance between the physical and spiritual realm. As you scrap negativity and conflict, you can rest, spend time with family, and heal. '666' may be warning you that you are too focused on the material world, and your spiritual needs are not being met. When this imbalance happens, you give into obsessive thoughts and lose harmony. Therefore, '666' is not so much an omen of bad luck, but as a word of encouragement from your angels to be grateful and patient during discouraging times.

What Your Future Holds: A chance to spiral or transform.

What You Can Do:

- Take time off for a spa trip, staycation, hiking, or mini-vacation.
- Rework your schedule to fit in time for self-care and family life.
- Get in touch with the spiritual: meditate, pray, read scriptures, or practice yoga.
- Mute social media to minimize distractions and negativity.

6666

A Major Message for You: Stop focusing on the material and nourish your soul.

If '6666' emerges as a pattern in your life, your angels are encouraging you to remain positive, although you may feel like things are spiraling out of control. With positive thinking and the pursuit of balance in your life, you can gain the strength and wisdom to overcome all odds. Linked to the energies of six (6+6+6+6= 24 = 2+4 = 6), '6666' is a friendly warning to stay on track, be honest about your feelings, elevate your spirit, and take care of your body. Since the Universe reads your vibrations, it is crucial to keep your vibrations positive and focused on manifestation. During this time, therefore, you may need to care for yourself even more by muting social media, encouraging intentional positivity, and taking time to develop spiritually. Your angels may also be using '6666' to warn about toxic, addictive, or obsessive behavior that erodes your mental and spiritual well-being. The good news is that you are not alone. Be sure to ground yourself with positive friendships and relationships, healing rifts, and nurturing others around you.

What Your Future Holds: You will overcome obstacles.

What You Can Do:

- Meditate or practice yoga for increased mindfulness.
- Rework your schedule to maintain a better balance of work and rest.
- Speak and write positivity into your life with meaningful, intentional sentences.
- Serve others through volunteer work.
- Analyze physical and mental habits, looking for toxic or obsessive behavior.

REPEATING SEVENS

77

A Major Message for You: Be confident! You have been blessed.

Your angels are cheering you onward! '77' emerging in your life should be seen as encouragement from your angel guides. It is a call to be confident and prepared for the next new phase of growth. You did well, but your angels are also giving you a heads-up— change is coming. This is because '77' is linked to five's energies (7+7 = 14 = 1+4 = 5). As a result, this is a time for celebration and preparation. Set your intentions at this time by writing or speaking with the aid of precise visualization to enhance your manifestation techniques. It is also a good idea to study spiritual practices and increase your knowledge of the Universe. As you develop your spiritual self, you will cultivate positive relationships with your angel guides and other areas of life, such as romance. '77' tells you to feel confident that you are on the right path, but don't forget to keep moving forward. Take advantage of this number right now to achieve manifestation because this number's power can fade with inaction.

What Your Future Holds: Manifestation of your goals and dreams.

What You Can Do:

- Practice meditation to increase mindfulness and focus.
- Study spiritual materials—prayers, meditations, scriptures, and songs.
- Use the manifestation techniques in Chapter 7 to maximize manifestation potential.
- Connect and communicate with your spirit guides and Ascended Masters.

777

A Major Message for You: You are in sync with the Universe!

'777' is a shout-out, reassuring you that you are properly aligned with the Universe and your internal truths. During this time, your heart is open to higher consciousness, spiritual enlightenment, and manifestation. Now is the time to recover balance and perspective, especially in assessing material possessions, needs, and desires. '777' signals a time when we are better able to evaluate our lives properly. With this new perspective comes new possibilities, particularly in the spiritual realm. Since '777' is linked to three (7+7+7=21 = 2+1 = 3), energies of creativity and communication point to a shift that is required on your part. Pay attention to the communication of angel guides through scriptures, synchronicities, and meditation sessions. As this spiritual evolution begins to take effect, you will start to fully understand the support of your angels and the reality of manifestation. As spiritual possibility becomes a reality, abandon negativity and get ready to access your spiritual intuition for the next phase of your life.

What Your Future Holds: Chances to achieve further spiritual enlightenment.

What You Can Do:

- Get in touch with the spiritual: meditate, pray, read scriptures, and practice yoga.
- Research spiritual practices and beliefs that will enhance your growth.
- Journal.
- Visualize, fully, the things and people you want to see in your life.

7777

A Major Message for You: It's time to reap the benefits of your hard work.

If you notice '7777' emerge as a synchronicity in your life, this is a promise of success from your angels. They have seen how hard you have been working and want to assure you that your rewards are waiting right around the corner. Now is the time to take on projects you've always wanted to do but put off for another day. Access the miracles waiting in '7777' because you are destined for great things with this number. Since you are in the lucky period of your life, it is also an excellent time to help others, sharing your wisdom and abundance. Linked to one (7+7+7+7= 28 = 2+8= 10 = 1+0= 1), '7777' tells you that now is the time to take control of your life and take advantage of an opportunity, and come out on top. It's an excellent time to build on wealth and maintain career momentum as well. '7777' also encourages you to meditate and connect to the collective unconscious for perspective and self-discovery to work on spiritual development. Certain aspects of your life need attention, such as your health or family life, so use these positive vibrations as opportunities for personal growth.

What Your Future Holds: Rewards for your efforts: Wealth, relationship, and career-related blessings.

What You Can Do:

- Start a new project, hobby, or skill.
- Make some financial decisions with an eye on long-term success.
- Meditate or practice yoga for increased mindfulness.
- Rework your schedule to maintain a better balance of work and rest.

REPEATING EIGHTS

88

A Major Message for You: Open yourself to abundance.

The emergence of '88' in your life as a synchronicity promises you that material blessings are on the way. However, our spirits and minds must be open to abundance through attitudes and practices encouraging receiving and giving. With responsibility and diligence, you will weather the difficult times and not only survive but thrive! '88' encourages you to remember that success and fulfillment are just around the corner. You only need to focus and persevere. As a result, you need to plan well, treat money with respect, practice gratitude, and make wise choices. Know that your angel guides are working to support your path to success. Just make sure that you are not swept away by greed or obsession with material gain on this journey. Linked to the energies of Number 7 (8+8=16 = 1+6= 7), '88' also reminds us that spirituality is directly related to the physical world. Our spiritual attitudes toward wealth and finances will affect our success. As a result, virtues such as discernment, abstinence, generosity, gratitude, and moderation will be rewarded. It would help if you worked on a positive relationship and attitude towards money. As a result, your financial aspirations will be achieved through manifestation.

What Your Future Holds: Material blessing is on the way.

What You Can Do:

- Manage debt and stay on top of bills.
- Spend wisely and budget.
- Stay focused and on track with well-paced scheduling and optimized workspaces.
- Speak and write specific financial aspirations into your life with meaningful, intentional sentences.

888

A Major Message for You: It's time to face your Karma!

You are at the cusp of a new phase in your life. At this time, you are poised to receive rewards for all of your hard work. However, it is crucial to let go of negative thoughts and feelings to embrace the change that is brewing. This mental and spiritual readiness increases your rate of manifestation. Part of this process involves an attitude shift. '888' is encouraging you to act as if you already have the wealth you want. The Universe will notice your positive vibrations and bring the happiness you seek. Linked to the energies of six (8+8+8=24 = 2+4= 6), '888' encourages you to embrace balance and stability, particularly in terms of material wealth. With healthy boundaries set around your attitude towards wealth, you are ready to receive material and spiritual abundance. Since '888' is a Karmic Number, your spiritual well-being plays an integral part in the outcome of your rewards. At this time, you should improve your Karma by blessing others and developing yourself spiritually. Since this is the start of a new phase filled with its challenges, make sure to take the time to celebrate and enjoy the fruits of your labor. During this period, you should tap into new talents and skills to start new projects or tackle a new job or relationship. A world of opportunity is ready to be discovered!

What Your Future Holds: Karma returns, either good or bad.

What You Can Do:

- Speak and write finance-related positivity into your life with meaningful, intentional sentences.
- Start a new project, hobby, or skill.
- Use meditation, prayer, and journaling to navigate and work through your Karma.
- Celebrate the rewards you are experiencing now.

8888

A Major Message for You: You are getting what you are owed.

Angels have got your back! The presence of '8888' in your life should reassure you that a large amount of good fortune is coming! You are finally reaping the rewards of all that hard work you have been doing. There will be a positive change in your luck, but you need to be diligent, focused, and persevering to make the most of these positive vibrations. Now is not the time to dwell on past pains or grievances. Instead, embrace positive thinking and the abundance that is starting to arrive. Reach out to coworkers, friends, and family to share in your good fortune. Now is the time to network and prepare for the next phase. Another essential aspect to consider is renewal. With the vibrations of '8888', use this opportunity to renew spiritual vows and rediscover your spiritual gifts. Linked to the energies of five (8+8+8+8= 32 = 3+2= 5), '8888' holds a promise of positive change, particularly in terms of finances. It's time to leverage personal freedom and material accumulation energies to achieve financial stability and prepare for the next set of challenges ahead. Stay strong with the knowledge that the Universe has your back. Don't be afraid! Push your limits!

What Your Future Holds: Good fortune and financial windfall are around the corner.

What You Can Do:

- Through journaling and other forms of therapy, process grudges, and traumas.
- Pursue positive life choices and habits on a day-to-day basis.
- Visualize, fully, the end product of your projects and dreams.
- Network thoughtfully.

REPEATING NINES

99

A Major Message for You: Don't delay! The time for your life mission has come.

If you notice '99' showing up as a pattern in your life, see this as a wake-up call from your angels. It is an alarm bell letting you know that your chance to fulfill your soul's mission has come. The energies of '99' are deeply action-oriented, pushing you to follow the plan the Universe has for you courageously. You should not delay. Change is coming, but don't be afraid! You are a lightworker, someone who has received the vital job of serving humanity and making the world a better place. '99' appears during serious decision-making times. When it appears, it is time to take action and pursue ways to do good. As you pursue proactive energies, you take ownership of and become empowered through your life's mission. Since '99' has extra hidden nine powers (9+9=18 = 1+8= 9), it is a number of completion and ascension, challenging you to trust your spiritual intuition and higher powers for guidance. As you release attitudes and things you don't need, you will be better able to practice self-love, develop self-control, and fully commit to your life purpose.

What Your Future Holds: Serious decision-making time.

What You Can Do:

- Get in touch with the spiritual: meditate, pray, read scriptures, and practice yoga.
- Serve others through volunteer work or charitable giving.
- Minimize your belongings.
- Speak and write spiritual positivity into your life with meaningful, intentional sentences.

999

A Major Message for You: Learn from the past to move fearlessly into your future.

'999' announces the end of a cycle and the beginning of another. Don't worry! The Universe is planning and preparing something great for you. Now is the time to appreciate all of the hard work and rewards you have gained through your past experiences. As another door opens, you can take this time to look back and analyze the bigger picture of your life. Tap into your inner power and embrace the spiritual maturity that is happening. As your soul-mission comes into view, this may be your call to lightwork, which involves healing the Earth and helping others. Like '99', '999' has hidden 'nine' energies (9+9+9=27 = 2+7= 9) which amplifies the message of spiritual completion and ascension. However, sometimes we allow our past experiences to define us and our future solely. '999' reminds us that we are more than our failures or traumas. It challenges us to jettison our fears and pains and embrace our spiritual future. In turn, our pursuit for authenticity and elevation will inspire and support others.

What Your Future Holds: Another phase of your life is starting.

What You Can Do:

- Pursue visions of your next step through numerological calculations, as well as other spiritual practices and rituals.
- Fully visualize new projects and dreams.
- Through journaling and other forms of therapy, let the past go.
- Review your meditations, journal entries, and life choices to analyze the big picture of your life.

9999

A Major Message for You: Time to understand your life purpose.

It's time to tap into divine wisdom. The emergence of '9999' in your life is trying to help you channel your energies toward positive interactions with the world through light-work or positive leadership. '9999' lets you know that you are meant to help people and heal the world. You are unique, a beacon of hope working out good Karma and positive synchronicity. Don't be afraid. Blessings are coming. We just need to prepare for them by protecting our energy from negativity and surrounding ourselves with beauty and light. If you are currently facing depressing or negative input from others or life circumstances, work practically toward solving these issues to utilize the vibrations of '9999' properly. Like '99' and '999', '9999' holds the ultimate hidden Number 9

(9+9+9+(= 36 = 3+6= 9), pointing to spiritual completion and purpose. Self-sacrificing, compassionate, patient, and optimistic, you work for the welfare of humanity, seemingly at the cost of your existence. However, because of your deep connections to the spiritual heart of the Universe, you will never run dry. Your angels are working closely with you as you end one phase and begin another. Your cup is over-flowing.

What Your Future Holds: Opportunity to heal the world.

What You Can Do:

- Serve others through volunteer work or charitable giving.
- Speak positivity into other people's lives through works of art, words of encouragement, gifts of generosity, and charitable work.
- Stay focused and on track with well-paced scheduling and optimized workspaces.
- Meditate or practice yoga for increased mindfulness and spiritual sensitivity.

LISTENING TO ANGEL NUMBERS

With meditative and other spiritual practices, you will better tune your soul to listen to the promptings of the Universe. The next time you turn on the radio, call a number, look at the clock, or notice a figure in your bank account, you may see a recurring number that looks specific and special. Take it as a sign from your angel guides, which you must consider during times of meditation.

One important thing to keep in mind is that the interpretations provided for the core numbers and repeating angel numbers in Chapters 3 and 4 are standard interpretations that can be helpful starting points for numerological interpretation. However, your life and the numbers you see are specific to you, so be sure to think about your numbers and the aspects of your circumstances to apply these interpretations best. There are no hard and fast rules for numerological interpretation on a personal and practical level.

The world of numerology is vast, complex, and incredibly personalized, but you have all you need to explore it. With the information we have covered thus far, with support and wisdom from the Universe. With confidence in your angels, you are ready to tackle other numerical sequences and combinations to manifest your dreams and desires!

5

NUMBER SEQUENCES AND COMBINATIONS

Imagine yourself calling home from work. You have been called away suddenly to a new worksite, and you don't know when you'll be home. Unfortunately, reception is poor, and you can only hear static with the occasional burst of someone talking. There's no way you are going to be able to tell your partner that you'll be home late.

Like the static of poor reception interrupting your conversation, distractions and conflicts bombarded us daily, drowning out the voices of our angels. Noticing synchronicities can be difficult at times, so receiving a core number or a repeating angel number is particularly helpful, meaningful, and, therefore, powerful. However, what are you going to do when you receive a random number?

Analyzing two or more-digit angel numbers may seem impossible, so you might be tempted to rely on websites for the interpretation of your numbers. However, I firmly believe that the best interpretations of angel numbers come from within oneself. I hope to show you some practical ways to analyze and interpret your own unique numbers, regardless of what they contain. This way, you will not only be empowered to interpret angel numbers for yourself, but you will also be able to help others gain wisdom in their study of angel numbers as well.

GENERAL TIPS

In Chapter 2, we looked at multi-digit numbers that hold complex meanings. Yet, the basic descriptions of these numbers are derived from understanding the "core numbers."

While understanding core numbers is crucial, arrangements or patterns are equally important. If you notice repeating (2020) or sequential numbers (2345), these usually tell you that your spirit guides are encouraging you on the path you have chosen. These numerical arrangements reveal that you are pursuing properly aligned instincts and are on track.

Numerological arrangement is vital for numbers with three or more digits. Seuss suggests that the first number can be seen as the "causal number," explaining how you have arrived at where you are now. The last number is seen as the 'effectual' or "process number," showing what to expect or how to make the most of the vibrations of the angel number. Suess and other numerological experts, including Padre and Doreen Virtue, agree that the middle numbers are the core values of complex angel numbers.

Studying other numerologists' interpretations may be helpful, particularly as they may see patterns in numbers that you are not familiar with or haven't noticed yet. For example, in her article, "Angel Numbers Guide: Why You Keep Seeing Angel Number Sequences," Katherine Hurst offers some observations about common number combinations, such as zero and four (2019). Here are a few examples:

- 2 & 6—Abundance is on the way.
- 8 & 3—Take care of yourself and work on replenishing your energy.
- 0 & 4—You are deeply loved and needed in this world.

While these kinds of guides are beneficial for potential insight, you must give yourself personal, analytical freedom to leverage your angel numbers' unique potential. I cannot emphasize how important it is for you to meditate, consult your spirit guides, and listen to your intuition!

BASIC APPROACHES TO MULTI-DIGIT ANGEL NUMBERS

Let's have a look at the basic steps to breaking down and analyzing multi-digit angel numbers. We will be using a 5-step process distilled from various sources, including Virtue and Brown, Padre, and Seuss.

First Step: Separate each digit and look at each number's "core number" meaning. If you receive '924' as your angel number, for example, you should use the information in Chapter 3 to define 'nine,' 'two,' and 'four.'

- 'Nine' energies are summed up by forgiveness, compassion, community, reward, lethargy.
- The energies of 'two' are summed up by sensitivity, compromise, harmony, balance, overly compliant.
- 'Four' energies are summed up by stability, tradition, hard work, security, unchangeability.

Second Step: Take note of the arrangement of these three numbers. Note that 'nine' may be potentially identifying the context or cause of this angel number. Think about how the energies of 'two' may be defining the main drive or point of the angel number. Identify how 'four' may be the results of 'nine' and 'two' or might be an explanation of how 'two' should work through your life.

- 'Nine' as cause number: You are emerging from the end of one cycle and are entering another.
- Two' as core number: You are loved and supported by the Universe, spirit guides, deceased loved ones, and your earthly community.
- 'Four' as effect number: Get down to business, and use skills and organization to achieve your dreams.

Third Step: Research and consider the additional meanings of other number combinations within your angel number. These combinations may contain different directions you can consider as well.

- 92: You are moving from a stage of spiritual completion and are being encouraged to continue pursuing spiritual harmony and balance.
- 24: As you focus on your work (both spiritual and physical), your angel guides support you.

Fourth Step: Calculate the cumulative (or hidden) number of your angel number by adding all of the numbers together and then adding the sum as well. However, if the cumulative sum is '11', '22', or '33', don't continue with the calculation since these numbers are significant and powerful (Seuss, 2021).

$$(924 = 9+2+4 = 15^* = 1 + 5 = 6)$$

As stated previously, if the number '15' were '11', '22', or '33', some numerologists would recommend stopping your calculations, but it really is up to you! In this calculation, our cumulative (or hidden) core number is six, which relates to the balance and reassessment of one's priorities.

Fifth Step: Meditate and analyze the various meanings and applications found in all of these numbers. Synthesize what you have discovered into intentional messages of positivity and manifestation.

A potential reading for '924' could be: As you emerge from the end of one cycle and enter another one, know that you are loved and supported by your angels. With this knowledge, embrace empowerment and healthy balance within life as you continue working on your path to manifestation and success.

One way you could turn this into intentional speech for manifestation techniques is to add 'I' to these statements and personalize the expression of the numbers' energies. For example: "I am loved! I am ready for a new phase of life! I embrace power and balance as I manifest my dreams!"

Now that you know the five basic steps to breaking down and analyzing multi-digit angel numbers let's practice by looking at a few more numbers.

TWO-DIGIT NUMBERS

Let's start with two different double-digit numbers: 20 and 78. Let's review the five steps to analyze 20 first.

Step One: We have to break '20' down into two separate core numbers—two and zero. 'Two' is summed up by the following descriptors: sensitivity, compromise, harmony, balance, and overly compliant. 'Zero' is best described as limitless, endless, anything, nothing, everything, and divine totality.

Step Two: With a two-digit number, the arrangement is less important because we can see both energies as being more or less equal or in harmony (since there are two numbers involved). In this case, we can say that the concepts of support found in 'two' are complemented equally by the limitlessness of 'zero.'

Step Three: Once again, we do not need to seek alternative combinations since only two numbers are involved. However, it is essential to note that 'zero' has the additional power of amplification, which, in this case, is increasing the energies of 'two.'

Step Four: The cumulative number of '20' is formulated by the following: 20 = 2+0 = 2. With the additional hidden number of 'two,' we get a triple amplification of two vibrations.

Step Five: Meditate and turn these discoveries into intentional speech, which you can use in journaling or manifestation techniques. An example: Embrace divine harmony and know you are loved. You are ready to take on anything! An example of intentional speech would be: "I am loved! I am ready to take on anything!"

Now, let's consider the number 78. Try to use the previous five steps to figure out your own interpretation of this number. Compare your conclusions with mine and appreciate the difference of vision we can all have about the same numbers.

Step One: Core number seven's energy is characterized by loneliness, mysticism, skepticism, enlightenment, and perfectionism. 'Eight' is linked to power, success, abundance, influence, and domination.

Step Two: Intellectual and spiritual enlightenment is linked to abundance and success.

Step Three: Nothing applicable for this number.

Step Four: The cumulative number of 78 can be formulated: $78 = 7+8 = 15 = 1+5 = 6$. The hidden energies of 'six' point to responsibility, family, and balanced living.

Step Five: Meditate and create an intentional speech from your angel number. Potential reading of 78 is: As you align with divine purpose on a spiritual level, you will gain abundance in the physical realm, providing you a balance of success and resources, spiritually and physically. A possible intentional statement would be: "I am ready to accept spiritual and physical abundance!"

THREE-DIGIT NUMBERS

Now that you have worked out the basics with core numbers, repeating numbers, and double-digits, tackling three-digit angel numbers should hopefully look less daunting. Let's take a look at a variation of the numbers we studied already: 202 and 781.

For '202', we notice right away that we have an interesting arrangement happening. First, we can note the core numbers, 'two' and 'zero,' and write down what they represent in general (see the previous example). Then, we can analyze the numerical arrangement. 'Two' is a causal number and an effectual number, while 'zero' features as the driving number. What this means is that harmony and awareness of love provide support while exploring the divine or one's options and lead to further awareness of support and confidence moving forward. If we use step 3 to break '202' down into double-digit numbers, we get '20' and '02', which reminds us that 'zero' is often used as an amplifier. Therefore, we have repeating twos, but we also have 'zero,' which should tell us that our angel guides really want us to pay attention to the energies of 'two.' Another calculation we should try out is the cumulative number. In this case, (202 =

2+0+2 = 4). 'Four' is linked to hard work, firm foundations, and stability.

To sum '202' up, we can interpret this angel number as great encouragement from your angels. They are letting you know that you are supported and loved and that you are connected to the divine or have limitless potential and should therefore start spreading the love and building firm foundations for a successful future. You could turn '202' into intentional posi-tivity: "I am loved. I have potential. It's time for me to share this love and work for my bright future."

Now, let's have a look at what messages '781' might hold. I encourage you to try breaking down and analyzing this number on your own before reading what conclusions to which I came.

Step One: Analyze the core numbers.

- Number 7's energy is characterized by loneliness, mysticism, skepticism, enlightenment, and perfectionism.
- Number 8's energy is characterized by power, success, abundance, influence, and domination.
- Number 1's energy is characterized by individuality, independence, initiative, determination, and selfishness.

Step Two: Note the arrangement of the core numbers.

- Seven as a causal number: "I am ending one cycle and beginning a new phase. I have achieved a form of spiritual awakening or enlightenment. I am complete."
- Eight as core number: "I am reaping the rewards of my hard work and Karma. Abundance is coming to me."
- One as an effectual number: "Through action, initiative, and determination, I will capitalize on my success as I take on new opportunities in the next stage of my life."

Step Three: Research other combinations of numbers found in '781'.

- 78: With spiritual alignment comes material abundance and success.
- 81: You are working hard, but abundance is right around the corner. Take this opportunity to keep going and press forward for new opportunities to succeed.

Step Four: Calculate the cumulative (hidden) number.

$$(781 = 7+8+1 = 16 = 1+6 = 7)$$

The hidden number of 'seven' points to completion and alignment with divine purpose. Your angels are pleased with the path you are taking!

Step Five: Meditate, interpret, and synthesize.

One way to interpret '781' could be: As you end this stage of growth, enjoy the abundance of rewards coming your way. Use this time to prepare for new opportunities and challenges coming ahead!

A great intentional statement you could write might be: "I am grateful for my spiritual and material abundance, present and future. I am ready for more opportunities to succeed!"

FOUR-DIGIT NUMBERS

Now that we have practiced with double and triple-digit numbers, it's time to tackle another set of large numbers. Don't worry, though! The process remains the same. Let's have a look at 2020 and 7814.

With '2020', we notice right away that we have a pattern in progress. When we break the number down, we have twos and zeros, with which we are now familiar. You can remind yourself what energies are found within twos and zeros in previous examples or in Chapter 3. As you may have guessed, we can look at the numerical arrangement next. The first digit can be read as 'causal' for four-digit numbers, the last digit is 'effectual,' and the middle digits as the "core drive." In '2020', the core is almost the same as in '202', focusing on the 'zero.' However, in this case, the 'zero' is amplifying another core number: the 'two.' In short, there is a heavy emphasis on establishing an emotional bond with your spirit guides and the divine, encouraging you to be brave as you make crucial decisions. Your awareness of love (cause) will lead to confidence and divine elevation (effect). The cumulative calculation of 2020 remains the same:

$$(2020 = 2+0+2+0 = 4)$$

There is an underlying encouragement to work hard, organize well, and be proactive in our lives, especially when it comes to decision-making. The repeating twos with the repeating zeros, therefore, are a powerful message from your angels to let you know that you are being supported during this time of decision-making. As you make deeper spiritual connections with the divine and your spirit guides, you will be better positioned to manifest your dreams into reality. An intentional statement around the number '2020' might be: "I am connected to the divine. I am ready for whatever is coming. Through my efforts, my dreams will come true." '2020' is a surprisingly encouraging message that should get us thinking about ways to become proactive in our journey of self-development and manifestation. What could '7814' teach us?

Step One: Analyze the core numbers.

- Number 7's energy is characterized by loneliness, mysticism, skepticism, enlightenment, and perfectionism.
- Number 8's energy is characterized by power, success, abundance, influence, and domination.
- Number 1's energy is characterized by individuality, independence, initiative, determination, and selfishness.
- Number 4's energy is characterized by stability, tradition, hard work, security, and unchangeability.

Step Two: Note the arrangement of the core numbers.

- Seven as a causal number: "I am ending one cycle and beginning a new phase. I have achieved a form of spiritual awakening or enlightenment. I am complete."
- Eight as core number: "I am reaping the rewards of my hard work and Karma. Abundance is coming to me."
- One as core number: "I am going to take the initiative, maximize all opportunities to capitalize on my success, and prepare for the next phase of my life."
- Four as an effectual number: "Through organization and diligence, I will work hard to secure important

foundations in my life, manifest my dreams, and share my successes with others around me."

Step Three: Research other combinations of numbers found in '7814'.

- 78: With spiritual alignment comes material abundance and success.
- 81: You are working hard, but abundance is right around the corner. Take this opportunity to keep going and press forward for new opportunities to succeed.
- 14: You may have the energy and passion for pursuing new challenges, but you also need organization and diligence to follow through and make the most of these opportunities.

Step Four: Calculate the cumulative (hidden) number.

$$(7+8+1+4 = 20 = 2+0 = 2)$$

With the cumulative energies of 'two,' this hidden number evokes finding harmony and balance in your life, as well as reassurance that your Higher Powers support you, angel guides, deceased loved ones, and your community. Pursuing '7814', therefore, may increase spiritual and physical balance in your life and provide resources and support for others around you. You can also see the hidden number of 'two' as encouragement from your angel guides. Focus on your work and the direction of '7814'.

Step Five: Meditate, interpret, and synthesize.

Overall, you could summarize the energy of '7814' as the following: After working so hard on spiritual and physical maturation, you have achieved some of your goals and should now celebrate! Enjoy the rewards of your efforts but be sure to use the energies and vibrations of success to maximize your ongoing efforts. With focus and hard work, you will use your accomplishments to better the world and achieve manifestation in many relationships.

You could transform this knowledge into a positive affirmation of what you believe is coming: "I am celebrating the results of my hard work! I am going to maximize these positive vibrations through continued success and ongoing efforts! With my angels, I will manifest my dreams!"

BEAUTIFUL COMPLEXITY

Angel numbers hold unique power and interpretations for all of us. If you need potent messages of positivity in your life, shorten these longer messages into shorter affirmations you can repeat or write to yourself.

When faced with challenges or complex decision-making, consulting your angel numbers can be a source of enlightenment and encouragement as you move forward in faith.

Although it is nice to have a resounding call from the Universe in the shape of repeating numbers, all numbers carry significant meaning and support from your angels.

With this chapter complete, I hope you feel more empowered, creative, and open to interpreting your angel numbers and accessing the unique energies within them! Although online dictionaries and numerological knowledge are helpful, you don't need to settle for generalized ideas or a "one-size-fits-all" interpretation of your angel numbers. These messages have been brought to you loud and clear. It's time for you to discover them for yourself!

CONNECTION AND DISCONNECTION WITH ANGEL NUMBERS

The modern world feels like it is rushing all the time. Traffic speeds through our bustling cities. Stoplights feel like they take forever. Our phones are ringing all the time insistently. We can't turn them off, or else we will miss out on something. At some point, you might pause for a moment and wonder whether this constant rushing and bustling is the best way to connect with life and the world around you.

Is there another way to live our lives? Angel numbers would say 'yes.' The Universe is invested in helping you achieve a balance between the physical and spiritual realms, guiding you to inner peace as well as outer gain. Without spiritual abundance, material possessions and success will feel stale and hollow—or even impossible to achieve.

With the help of angel numbers, not only will you be able to manifest what you need and desire, but you will also know how to best treasure these gifts and talents. The key is to connect with your angel numbers, but perhaps you haven't yet noticed synchronicities in your life. Or, having seen them, you are unsure of what to do next. Maybe you are no longer seeing them. By the end of this chapter, I hope that you will be able to begin your journey with angel numbers and implement practical strategies to enhance your spiritual awareness.

WHY AM I DISCONNECTED FROM ANGEL NUMBERS?

When you overhear people sharing their experiences with angel numbers, you might be feeling discouraged and envious. Why aren't you connecting with angel numbers? There are many reasons why this may be happening, and not all these reasons are negative. A key point to take away from this section is to work on your spiritual awareness and attitude because with openness, optimism, and gratitude, angel numbers will more likely emerge.

New to Numerology?

One reason why you may not yet have noticed angel numbers in your life is simply that you never knew that you could notice patterns. If you are entirely new to numerology and have not yet seen synchronicity in your life, don't panic! You may have seen a couple of numbers pop up but have since forgotten them because people around you (or society in general) encouraged you to regard these occurrences as coincidences. All you need to do is let your angels know, through prayer or meditation, that you are open to speaking with them. You may have to assess your attitudes to root out negative emotions, such as bitterness, anger, or cynicism. Once you have processed these emotions, you are ready to begin the journey toward self-development and manifestation alongside your angels.

Suddenly No Longer Seeing Angel Numbers?

If you have abruptly stopped seeing angel numbers, this may be due to a variety of reasons. For example, you may not have asked to see them more or have not aligned yourself properly to your core values and truths. As stated in Chapter 2, sometimes we try to pursue truth in angel numbers. Yet, deep down, we do not believe in, respect, or love ourselves properly and are therefore unable to tap into the energies of the Universe.

Another reason may be that sometimes, to achieve a new level of spiritual awakening, we are called to persevere and develop faith. Even during these times, when our angel numbers seem to have disappeared, it is essential to know that they always exist, embedded in the fabric of the cosmos in the same way that our angels always stand by us. During these periods of silence, don't be afraid. Continue to meditate and focus on your work until your angel numbers reappear!

This phenomenon can also indicate that the Universe and your angels are working on remodeling your destiny, which means that new angel numbers are coming your way. As mentioned before, it may seem to take time to see this as an opportunity to grow in spiritual resilience and strength. Your angels haven't given up! Don't give up either.

Lastly, sometimes angel numbers abruptly disappear because you are on the path you are supposed to be following for now. Although the Number 7 (or other repeating angel numbers using 'seven') can be a direct message of encouragement, angel numbers will often recede when you are on the right track. I believe this usually happens because your angels want you to remain focused on the task you have been given and not get overwhelmed or distracted by other upcoming events or possibilities. Practice patience and believe in your angels, as they will let you know what to do next when the time is right.

Rarely Seeing Angel Numbers?

As mentioned before, angel numbers are meant to be unique, meaningful, and powerful messages from the Universe to you, often brought to your attention thanks to the help of your spirit guides. However, these messages could lose impact if they were constantly popping up everywhere. Your angels know precisely what you are going through and what messages you need to see. If they have a warning or important announcement to make, rest assured that they will get you to notice!

If you feel like your angel messages have almost all but disappeared, there may be an obstacle lowering your vibrations. Nowadays, we are bombarded with bad news, rumors, and clickbait. Perhaps it is time for you to undergo a spiritual and mental cleansing with a fast from social media. If social media has become a severe addiction or distraction in your life, you should consider going on a spiritual retreat. Set aside more extended periods for personal interaction with the world. Here are a few practical things you can do to minimize the impact of the material world on your spiritual senses:

- Only use your phone between set hours (for example, between 9 a.m. and 5 p.m.).
- Practice analog forms of scheduling and journaling, such as bullet journaling.
- Mute your phone. Turn off the app notifications, except for your text and calling apps (for emergencies).
- Set aside at least one day of the week as a rest period, where you can mute your phone, interact with friends, do housework, reconnect with nature, or read.

- On your day of rest, be yourself. Don't worry about makeup or looking good. It's healthy to appreciate your whole self without external pressures.
- When listening to music, choose classical, ambient, or New Age tracks, which will create a positive atmosphere in your home.

Here are some examples of behavior, feelings, or thought that will lower your vibration and make it much more difficult to receive messages from you angels:

- Any negative thought or talk
- Frustration
- Fear
- Being controlling
- Stress
- Impatience
- Anger
- Being judgmental
- Thoughts of lack or scarcity

When you catch yourself thinking or feeling any of these ways, turn to gratitude. This will snap you out of that negative behavior. The goal is to have flow in your life to keep you aligned and in a high vibration. Set your intention and remain positive. There is good in every situation, you just need to change your perspective and have faith.

Once you have disentangled yourself from the rat race of social media and the world around you, you should be able to hear your angels once again. Be sure to pray and meditate, asking them to send more angel numbers your way. After all, sometimes we rarely see angel numbers simply because we forget to ask for more!

Have Your Angel Numbers Changed?

Sometimes, there will be a period of silence, and then you will notice another number emerging as synchronicity in your life. Do not be concerned, but celebrate! It is a sign that your angel guides want you to invest energy into another area of your life. For example, you may have been focusing on spiritual work related to your attitude because of seeing 126 in your life. Now they need you to focus on some practical aspects and reveal another number, like 168. You should see changing angel numbers as encouragement and support from your angel guides. They are working hard alongside you to manifest your dreams and are willing to put in extra effort to make sure you are achieving a life of healthiness and balance!

Standing on the Peak

Another sporadic reason you appear to have disconnected from your angel numbers is that you have received all the guidance you need, and you need to keep doing what you are doing. Your angels are still there, supporting and loving you; however, they no longer need to bombard you with messages since you are accomplishing all that you desire.

Does this mean that you will never see angel numbers again in your life? Not necessarily. For the foreseeable future, your angels may simply choose to allow you to enjoy and pursue the life you are leading. If at any point, the Universe opens up a new door for you, your angels will be there to reconnect with and direct you through new angel numbers.

HOW CAN I CONNECT WITH MY ANGEL NUMBERS?

In the last section, I provided some practical ways to disconnect from the external world and reconnect with your angel numbers. This section will dive deep into practical activities, meaningful spiritual exercises, and affirmative attitudes you can embrace to better connect with your angels and angel numbers. Remember that your angels and angel numbers are always there, but you need to take an active part in the process of determining your life and destiny. **Angels need to be invited in. We have been given the gift of free will, they will not necessarily intervene without an invitation. Simply ask in prayer for their guidance daily.**

The Power of Meditation and Prayer

With the external world always clamoring for our attention, clearing your mind can be very difficult. After setting aside and muting your phone, take a seat in a sacred space you have set apart in your home and relax. Close your eyes and take deep breaths. While you are meditating, thoughts may arise. Allow them to form and then release them, returning to a quiet place. These thoughts are now with your angels, who will begin working on them with you.

Prayer is another form of training your thoughts and releasing your worries. It is scientifically proven that prayer can rewire your brain and is the best way to get you into a Theta state. **When in Theta state, you are in a high vibration and begin attracting the things you desire.**

If you struggle with keeping your visualizations specific or staying focused, writing your prayers out in a prayer journal can help as well. Don't worry about being formal or finding the right words. The Universe and your angels fully understand the energies behind your prayers.

In the beginning, it may be difficult for you to focus while meditating or praying, and perhaps forming words and thoughts will also be challenging. There are many resources available to help you channel your energies appropriately, such as the prayers and meditations I recommend in Chapter 8. Choose a prayer, poem, or quote I listed, read through it several times aloud, visualize what it looks like for you, and imagine yourself within the reality of that world. You can also write these powerful messages to yourself in your journal. In this way, words of positivity and encouragement will remain with you and form positive vibrations to which the Universe will respond.

Making Contact With Your Guides

Many people, such as Suzanne Giesemann, have significant experience and relationships with special spirits. With their help and guidance, you may be able to access higher consciousness and gain clear direction. Perhaps they will be able to discover an angel number with great power for you.

Another way for you to make contact with your angel guides is to start talking to them simply. At first, it may feel like a one-way conversation, but you will begin to notice returned messages through angel numbers, spiritual intuitions, or even an emotional feeling with time. When meditating, always allow for silence so that your angels can bring feelings or ideas forward that you would not have otherwise anticipated. Visualizing what your angel looks like can also be a significant step towards making contact as well.

Raising Your Awareness

Connecting with angel numbers requires awareness as well, not only of numerical patterns but also of accompanying thoughts and feelings. Take notice of emotions and sensations that pop out at you as being unique. Get into the habit of connecting patterns between numbers in your life and those found in nature.

For example, if you notice your alarm clock says '7:50', and then on the way to work, you see a license plate with '750' on it, don't dismiss it. Skepticism discourages your spiritual intuition and can prevent the appearance of angel numbers. Instead, keep an open mind, and over the next few days, watch for any recurrence of '750'. It may pop up in unexpected places—from an ad to a bank account statement. While waiting, be sure to connect with your angels through prayer.

Both physical and numerical awareness will not only encourage your heart but also prepare your spiritual senses for intuitions and guidance from the Universe.

Heeding the Call

While you are waiting for your angel numbers to appear (or reappear), your angel guides may be trying to show support and love towards you in other ways. They can speak to us in various ways that may first seem unusual to you. Some common signs of angel communication are buzzing or humming, unexpected fragrances, the taste of sweetness, goosebumps, a slight breeze, or emotional feelings of love and calmness.

Some people will experience other visual cues, including rainbows, feathers, flashes of light, patterns in clouds, coins, or special animals (ex: butterflies). When angel numbers are absent or changing, these visual cues may be a personal sign of encouragement, reminding you that your angels are present and are still working with you. When these moments happen, don't dismiss them, but embrace the encouragement and enlightenment they bring.

Dreamwork

Connecting with angel numbers and your angel guides are not limited to the waking world. If you notice numbers or hear messages in your dreams, make sure to write them down in your journal and meditate on them. As you progress in your dream journaling, you may begin to notice patterns or repeated messages to which you should pay close attention. These numbers and messages are powerful ways for your angels to connect with you.

How do you boost your dream life? John Rampton, in his article, "8 Ways to Improve Sleep by Enhancing your Dreams", looks at ways to improve your sleep and dream state. Some practical steps to give your melatonin levels boost could be:

- Keeping a consistent sleep schedule.
- Reduce external stimulants—caffeine, light, TV rays.

- Eat food that raises melatonin levels: almonds, sunflower seeds, cherries, flaxseeds, tomatoes, ginger, bananas, barley, and oats.
- Ensure that your mattress provides you adequate support and comfort.
- Don't overdose on melatonin supplements.
- Exercise daily and eat well.
- Meditate before going to bed.
- Tell yourself that you will dream and will remember the dream.

Hopefully, some of these tips will aid you in your journey into the collective unconscious, the Universe, and yourself!

Setting Aside Sacred Spaces

Self-awareness is one of the essential steps to a more balanced life. Your angel guides will often use angel numbers to help you gain perspective on things you consider to be normal. One very 'normal' aspect of your life may be the spaces of your home. Look around your home, and start to explore the energies of your living space. Is it conducive to positive vibrations? Here are some suggestions for creating sacred space and better vibrations in your home:

- To enhance meditation sessions, ensure you have dim lighting or candles available.
- Burn incense or diffuse essential oils, such as rosemary or mint. These can help you relax during meditation.
- Practice the art of feng shui.
- Declutter and embrace a life of comfy minimalism.
- Decorate with tastefully and strategically placed crystals, gems, or minerals, such as celestite, selenite, and Angelite.
- Enhance your space with beautiful music, such as chimes, singing bowls, crystal bowls, and ambient sound.
- Decorate with tastefully and strategically placed prisms, light reflectors, and angel figurines.
- Bring nature indoors with planters, garlands, wreaths, and bouquets.
- Separate your workspaces from your living and meditating spaces.

The key to connecting with the spiritual self is creating a sacred space in which to envelope yourself. Protected from the pressures, stresses, and rat race of modern life will enable you to connect with your angel guides even more efficiently.

Return to Nature

As mentioned above, bringing nature into your home is a good step towards realigning your soul and connecting with your angels. Hiking in the wild or cottaging in the woods will provide even deeper immersion than a walk around the block. These opportunities will allow you to disconnect easier and channel your energies into healthier, more balanced paths. As your vibrations sync with the natural world, your spirit will become more open to the energies of the Earth and the Universe.

If you are living in the country, aligning with nature may feel more familiar to you. However, if you live in the city, you may need to be more intentional with bringing nature indoors. Finding peaceful parks, bird or butterfly sanctuaries, aquariums, and planetariums can help orient you towards more nature-focused energies. Gardening or volunteering with tree-planting initiatives is another excellent way for you to reconnect and give back to nature.

Journey With Journaling

Journaling can sometimes seem like a yawn fest, but it doesn't have to be that way. More than scheduling or recounting your day, journaling can provide you with another way to communicate with your angels, as well as properly process your emotions and thoughts. How are you going to leverage your meditative time with journaling?

- Write a letter—but keep it casual and informal. You are talking to your angel! They are friends, so don't be shy!
- Be honest and write down what you really want and how you feel deep down.
- Ask questions. It's OK to admit that you don't have answers right now.
- Avoid predesigned scheduling books. Choose a journal that allows you to work and visualize in your own way. While lined notebooks are helpful, consider trying out dot grid or dual half-blank/half-lined paper.
- Write about specific topics or feelings in regards to a particular issue or situation. Don't be vague. Use this time to explore all facets of a problem.
- Ask for help and be specific with that which you need help. Read this prayer aloud after you are finished writing it.
- Draw mind maps as you pursue solutions to a problem. Your angels may prompt you as you look at your options!
- Practice hypnagogic/hypnotic writing and drawing as a manifestation technique. These forms of writing will deepen your connection with the spiritual world, as well as form habits of positivity in your mind. You will begin to get the answers you are searching for.

Getting into the habit of journaling will not only provide you with more confidence to approach your day or assess your schedule it will also deepen communication with your angel guides. Through your writing, your angel guides will better understand your heart and your needs and may even place ideas and suggestions in your mind while you are brainstorming. Your journey to self-discovery is about to begin!

Change From the Inside Out

When it comes to leveraging the power of your angel numbers, working on your spiritual and mental health is paramount. Practicing gratitude, acceptance, faith, positivity, and confidence produces the best vibrations for receptivity to your angels and the Universe. As your spiritual faith and positivity grow, your spiritual awareness will increase, and you will become more receptive to angel numbers. Not only should you think affirmatively about situations in your life, but also about yourself.

While you journal, meditate and pray, implement some of these intentional affirmations as encouragement and connection:

- Focus on "I am" statements, which form positive images of yourself and your perspective on life.
- Be honest with the external and internal struggles you are facing.

- Speak words of love to yourself. Focus on meditations of love and support
- List things that you are thankful for already.
- Write intentional, positive sentences based on your angel numbers, using patterns, like "I will. . ." or "I am. . .".
- Meditate on the immovable obstacles in your life, and thank the Universe for providing you with an opportunity to grow.

CONNECTION WITH THE UNIVERSE

Now that you have all the tools for connecting with your angel numbers, it is time to use your angel numbers' energies, vibrations, and guidance. With proper application of the Law of Attraction and direction from your angel numbers, you will achieve the manifestation of your dreams. With prayer, positivity, and communication, you will discover your angel numbers. They are waiting for you!

7

MANIFESTATION WITH ANGEL NUMBERS

You now have all the ingredients you need to make your dreams come true. With knowledge about the Law of Attraction, manifestation, the energies of angel numbers, angel number calculations, and the steps to communicating with your angel guides, you are more than ready to start making your dreams come true. . . Well, almost. As any good baker knows, you need more than amazing ingredients to bake a cake. A great recipe is also required.

When it comes to using the Law of Attraction to achieve manifestation, you can use many different techniques and methods to make the most of the vibrations of the angel numbers you have noticed. Although we know that the Universe and everything in it are vibrating at various frequencies, you might wonder how your angel numbers can connect you to your dreams and goals.

First, it is essential to remember that the Law of Attraction states: To attract the frequency of what you desire, you must align your own vibrations to match. Thankfully, we have the power to control what kinds of vibrations we exude, including the consistency (positive or negative) and frequency.

Second, we need to recognize the vital link between the Law of Attraction and manifestation. Manifestation involves reshaping yourself and the world around you to make your dreams and goals a reality. Generally, manifestation techniques draw on the Law of Attraction theories and focus on increasing your positivity and spiritual connection to the Universe. Turning the guidance and energies of angel numbers into intentional affirmations, you can influence your thoughts and actions, rethink your attitude, and channel your energy into positive life choices.

The good news is that there are many ways to alter your vibrations and draw on the power of the Law of Attraction and special manifestation techniques designed to maximize the potential within you and the energy of specific angel numbers.

BEST LAW OF ATTRACTION PRACTICES

At first, changing your vibrations and energies from negative to positive may seem difficult. However, in Chapter 6, you already started that journey by creating solid foundations for development and transformation, not only for yourself but also for your home and other environments around you. Here are some general tips I have distilled from Adams, Greater Minds, and Shanker in regards to leveraging the Law of Attraction:

- Be mindful of your thoughts—combat negativity through meditation and prayer.
- Self-reflection through journaling. Understand what you need vs. what you want. Let your angel numbers tell you what direction in which you should head
- Create mental pictures or works of art visualizing your goals in detail.
- Affirm yourself and your intentions, internally or externally, through writing or speaking.
- Use sticky notes, dream boards, vision boards, focus wheels, bujo techniques, manifest shopping lists to focus, remind, and reiterate your intentions.
- Start with a small manifestation project. Positivity often increases with confidence, so allow yourself to celebrate over small victories.
- Make things happen for yourself—don't just sit around and obsess. Remember to let your intentional

thoughts go out to the Universe and then be patient
and focus on what you can do in the moment.

- Write intentions in the present tense and with an
affirmative voice. Encourage yourself on this
journey!

METHODS TO ACHIEVE MANIFESTATION

Manifestation techniques are specific ways to meditate and
affirm the reality you want to see. These techniques use a
combination of the positivity found in the Law of Attraction
and the energies and guidance found in specific angel
numbers. Many popular manifestation techniques focus on
powerful repeating angel numbers, which you can access and
use whether or not they appear as synchronicities in your
life. However, if they are already showing up in numerological calculations or daily synchronicities, be sure to maximize on the directions given to you and use the power of
these special angel numbers to manifest your dreams.

I also believe that calculations discovered in your birthdate
or name or through synchronicities found in daily life can
also provide sources for intentional affirmation. As you read
through these specific manifestation techniques, you will
notice a pattern emerge, which you can then apply to other
angel numbers in your life.

The 222 Technique

The powerful vibrations of '222' encourage you: Trust in yourself and the goodness of the Universe! As a result, many people feel energized and better aligned to the Universe through the manifestation of the "222 Technique". This technique, relying on the amplification of angel number 'two', encourages positive relationships toward the things or people you desire and increases affirmations in your life. Follow the steps below to maximize your potential and develop your mind and heart in preparation for what the Universe has in store!

Step One: Pick on goal or desire.

Step Two: Understand visualize it very precisely and clearly.

Step Three: Create an affirmative sentence.

Step Four: Write it 22 times once a day for two days straight.

Step Five: While writing, meditate on and visualize the words you are writing.

Step Six: End your manifestation sessions with a 'thank-you'!

The 555 Technique

The transformative vibrations of '555' have an announcement for you: Great change is coming! Make it happen!

Using the "555 Manifestation Technique", people wield the amplified angel number 'five' powerful energies, leading to rapid change or extreme transformation. If you can let go of the past and subconscious negative beliefs, you will be ready (both spiritually and physically) for what the Universe is about to bring. Follow the steps below if you are prepared to embrace not only your dreams but also the significant changes that will happen in the process and as a result of manifestation:

Step One: Pick on goal or desire.
Step Two: Understand visualize it very precisely and clearly.
Step Three: Create an affirmative sentence.
Step Four: Write it 55 times once a day for five days straight.
Step Five: While writing, meditate on and visualize the words you are writing.
Step Six: End your manifestation sessions with a 'thank-you'!

The 369 Technique

Drawing on the universal power of '369', also known as "The Divine Number," the "369 Manifestation Technique" harnesses the limitless ability of these three spiritual numbers to align your soul and manifest your dreams. Tesla is famous for his obsession with the numbers 'three', 'six,' and 'nine.' This is mainly due to a mathematical phenomenon that is observable when using sequences of vortex math. Unlike other numbers, they do not appear within the standard sequence that begins with 'one'. However, 'nine' does not show up when starting a vortex math sequence starting with 'three' or 'six', either! 'Nine' is truly set apart from all other numbers, so it is considered by many to be a very spiritual or individual number, often representing enlightenment and freedom. Follow the steps below if you are ready to access the energies of the divine to manifest your dreams and achieve spiritual awakening:

Step One: Pick one goal or desire.

Step Two: Understand and visualize it very precisely and clearly.

Step Three: Create an affirmative sentence.

Step Four: Write it three times in the morning.

Step Five: Write it six times around noon.

Step Six: Write it nine times in the evening.

Step Seven: While writing, meditate on and visualize the words you are writing.

Step Eight: End your manifestation sessions with a 'thank-you'!

GENERAL TIPS FOR MANIFESTATION PRACTICES

By now, you may have noticed a pattern in all of the manifestation techniques. Most manifestation work relies on the power of belief, faith, and positivity. Drawing on the Law of Attraction and the energies of a particular angel number, manifestation works best when your heart and desires align with other Universe elements. Let's look at some general tips for manifestation practices. Some of these suggestions reaffirm approaches mentioned in Chapter 6, using guidance from Through the Phases, Adams, Ducey, and Co Manifesting.

- When meditating, choose a space with high vibrational energies. Make sure to realign your home and workspace to elevate your vibrations.
- Visualizing requires focus and attention to detail. Don't be vague; instead, be specific.
- Use your five senses to realize what you want fully. Imagine interacting with it and allow yourself to feel the emotions you would have when using it.
- Research particular numerical calculations, like the Fibonacci Sequence Number or Personal Year Numbers, to recognize processes and external influences you need to consider while pursuing manifestation.
- When writing affirmation statements, use vivid imagery, specific, easy to remember words, present-tense verbs, and first-person voice ('I'). (Ex: "Thank you, Universe, for blessing me with a new job in finance.")

- Write your manifestations all at once by hand in your journal. Writing by hand (a more kinesthetic exercise) stimulates different areas of the brain.
- After finishing each manifestation session, end your time of writing with gratitude. Say 'thank-you' to your angels!
- When you are done with each manifestation session or have completed a phase of a manifestation technique, let it go. Focus on the present and what you can achieve now to better your life. Be patient and keep an eye out for other angel numbers or signs from the Universe!
- Work only on one affirmation at a time and keep your energies focused on one goal.

Keep an eye on your energy and thoughts while meditating or writing hypnotically. You want to ensure that you focus on visualizing, not allowing negative thoughts to creep in or distractions. Your vibrations need to stay positive, so approach manifestation techniques with excitement and joy. It is not a transaction. It is a conversation between you, your angels, and the Universe!

NOW WHAT?

As you have been reading this book, I hope that you feel more and more encouraged and empowered to begin your own journey to self-discovery and self-actualization. With a solid grasp of how to use the power of the Law of Attraction, the energies of angel numbers, and ways to connect with angel numbers, you have all the tools you need to achieve manifestation. As you grow in understanding your role within the Universe, as you connect with your angel or spirit guides, and as you begin to notice synchronicities in your life, I am praying that you will feel more emboldened to reach for what the Universe has planned for you.

8

INSPIRATION

Although you know how to interpret angel numbers and transform them into words of affirmation, sometimes, we can lose contact with our Truth. When this happens, our thoughts can turn to negativity and depressive thinking, which will repel the vibrations of the things in the Universe we desire. Without access to the Law of Attraction and with poorly visualized manifestation techniques, our angel numbers will be nothing more than signposts to a happier future. Only with cleansed and positively oriented spirits can we leverage the power of angel numbers and connect fully with the desires and promises of the Universe.

Perhaps recently, you have been feeling overwhelmed by external negativity and noise. Your voice feels silenced and ignored. During these periods, meditation and affirmation can be challenging to achieve, so it is essential to maintain sacred spaces within our homes and take breaks from the outside world. One way to transform our minds is to read or listen to uplifting songs, poems, and scriptures. In this chapter, I hope you can find meaningful words of encouragement that will enhance your meditation sessions.

INSPIRATION FROM THE GREATS

Poetic Infusion

- "If I Can Stop One Heart From Breaking" by Emily Dickinson
- "Hope Is The Thing With Feathers" by Emily Dickinson
- "Dreams" by Langston Hughes
- "The Road Not Taken" by Robert Frost
- "Ring Out, Wild Bells" by Lord Alfred Tennyson
- "A Psalm Of Life" by Henry Wadsworth Longfellow
- "Invictus" by William Ernest Henley
- "Still I Rise" by Maya Angelou
- "Don't Quit" by John Greenleaf Whittier
- "God's Grandeur" by Gerard Manley Hopkins

Quotes for Meditation

- **"The day science begins to study non-physical phenomena, it will make more progress in one decade than in all the previous centuries of its existence."—Nikola Tesla**

- "Yet, Ratnakara, a bodhisattva's buddha-field, is a field of positive thought. When he attains enlightenment, living beings free of hypocrisy and deceit will be born in his buddha-field."—Buddha (Vimalakirtinirdesa Sutra)

- "Knowing others is intelligence; knowing yourself is true wisdom. Mastering others is strength; mastering yourself is true power."—Lao Tzu.

- "The Lord is my shepherd, I lack nothing. He makes me lie down in green pastures, he leads me beside quiet waters, he refreshes my soul. He guides me along the right paths for his name's sake. Even though I walk through the darkest valley, I will fear no evil, for you are with me; your rod and your staff, they comfort me. You prepare a table before me in the presence of my enemies. You anoint my head with oil; my cup overflows. Surely your goodness and love will follow me all the days of my life, and I will dwell in the house of the Lord forever." —Psalm 25

- **"If you want to find the secrets of the universe, think in terms of energy, frequency, and**

vibration."—**Nikola Tesla**
- "To return to the root is to find peace. To find peace is to fulfill one's destiny."—Lao Tzu
- **"What one man calls God, another calls the laws of physics."—Nikola Tesla**
- "A person is what he or she thinks about all day long."—Ralph Waldo Emerson
- "The greatest discovery of my generation is that human beings can alter their lives by altering their attitudes of mind."—William James
- "Big things of the world / Can only be achieved by attending to their small beginnings."—Lao Tzu
- **"Your whole life is a manifestation of the thoughts that go on in your head."—Lisa Nichols**
- "Think the thought until you believe it, and once you believe it, it is."—Abraham Hicks
- "Keep your thoughts positive, because your thoughts become your words. Keep your words positive, because your behaviors become your habits. Keep your habits positive, because your habits become your values. Keep your values positive, because your values become your destiny."—Gandhi
- **"You manifest what you believe, not what you want."—Sonia Ricotti**
- "Nurture great thoughts, for you will never go higher than your thoughts."—Benjamin Disraeli
- "Thoughts become things. If you see it in your mind, you will hold it in your hand."—Bob Proctor

- "A bodhisattva's buddha-field is a field of meditation. When he attains enlightenment, living beings who are evenly balanced through mindfulness and awareness will be born in his buddha-field."
  —Buddha (Vimalakirtinirdesa Sutra)
- **"Nurture your mind with great thoughts, for you will never go any higher than you think."**
  —Benjamin Disraeli
- "For I know the plans I have for you," declares the Lord, "plans to prosper you and not to harm you, plans to give you hope and a future. Then you will call on me and come and pray to me, and I will listen to you. You will seek me and find me when you seek me with all your heart."— Jeremiah 29: 11-13
- "Every single second is an opportunity to change your life because in any moment you can change the way you feel."—Rhonda Byrne
- **"Every intention sets energy into motion, whether you are conscious of it or not."—Gary Zukav**
- "To accomplish great things we must not only act but also dream, not only plan but also believe."—Anatole France
- "A particle of Its bliss supplies the bliss of the whole Universe. Everything becomes enlightened in Its light. All else appears worthless after a sight of that essence. I am indeed of this Supreme Eternal Self."
  —Vijnananka

CONCLUSION

You hold a key in your hand. Before you, stands a great oak door ready to be unlocked and opened. What lies beyond? Only you can tell that story. This is only the beginning.

Before, the Universe felt overwhelming, empty, and distant. The stars shining in the Milky Way appeared cold and far-off, immeasurable and vast. Beneath this sky, alone in the wilds, you are confronted once again with those nagging fears and questions: Do I matter? Do things happen for a reason? Why am I here? What's going to happen next?

Take comfort. You know the Truth now. You do matter. Things do happen for a reason. You are here for a special purpose only you can discover for yourself. Your future is bright, and with the help of your angel guides, you have the power to write your own story.

All you have to do is surrender to the vibrations of the Universe, align with your divine purpose, and tap into the power and energy of angel numbers.

BECOMING THE CHANGE

Unlocking the door, the steps before you are made clear.

Connect with your angel guides. Through prayer and meditation, reach out to the Universe and ask for help. Your angel guides are ready and waiting to work with you. No longer will you feel like your life meanders. A direction that is intended to give you your heart's desires and mobilize you as a lightworker will impact this world for the good.

Open your spirit and mind to the synchronicities prepared for you. As you shed skepticism and the hyper rationality of this materialistic age, your inner eye and intuition will be ready to discover the synchronicities hidden within the fabric of the cosmos. Upon discovering your special angel numbers, be sure to follow the guidance of your angel with courage, diligence, and optimism.

Practice the power of positivity within the Law of Attraction. Recognize and believe the Truth that we are all connected within the Universe. The vibrations within you can be channeled and focused positively through manifestation techniques and interpretation of angel numbers. When your inner soul is aligned correctly with the Universe, you will be ready to achieve manifestation.

Meditate and prepare yourself, physically and mentally, for manifestation. In the process of enhancing positivity in your life, you will find ways to bring beauty and light to your home, work, and relationships. Taking care of yourself, physically and mentally, will become second nature. As a result, it will become natural for you to counsel others and become a model for optimism and light.

Achieve your dreams with the help of your angel guides and manifestation techniques. Using this book, you will not only be able to interpret angel numbers, but you will also be able to discover (through calculations and mindfulness practices) ways to connect deeply with your angels. With the support of your angels, the energy of your angel numbers, and the provided manifestation practices, you will be able to achieve your dreams.

In the process, not only will you surprise yourself with creativity, courage, diligence, and intuition, but also with compassion, enlightenment, and peace. Not only will you own the car you want, find the partner or friendships you seek, thrive in the job you need, but you will also transform the world around you, one positive act at a time. Your loved ones and community will blossom under your care.

BEYOND THE DOOR

Gerard Manley Hopkins is one of England's most mystical and spiritual poets from the Victorian Era. Struggling for most of his life with questions surrounding his faith and sexuality, Gerard Manley Hopkins instead chose to pursue a life of contemplation.

Throughout Hopkins's life, poetry was a source of struggle and serenity, as he grappled with his gift for writing and the complex world of the Victorian times. However, within his poetry, we find a yearning to return to God's goodness as seen in nature. Looking to forests, stars, and birds, Hopkins discovered not only the supreme value of the Universe but his own as well.

You, too, have this chance. As you walk through the door, what kind of world do you want to rediscover? What truths are waiting to be found within you, within nature, within your meditations?

As we advance, I pray that your world will be turned upside down, your horizons are broadened, and your visions are filled with opportunity. Before you, the sun is rising. It is a new day.

 "And for all this, nature is never spent; There lives the dearest freshness deep down things; And though the last lights off the black West went Oh, morning, at the brown brink eastward, springs - Because the Holy Ghost over the bent World broods with warm breast and with ah! bright wings."

— HOPKINS, 2020

REFERENCES

Adams, A. (2020a, December 2). Kabbalah vs. Pythagorean Numerology: The Two Most Popular Forms Explained. The Sage Divine. https://thesagedi vine.com/kabbalah-vs-pythagorean-numerology/

Adams, A. (2020b, December 2). Use Numerology to Manifest - Influence Your Life with Numbers. The Sage Divine. https://thesagedivine.com/ how-to-use-numerology-to-manifest/

Adams, A. (2021a). Angel Numbers. The Sage Divine. https://thesagedivine. com/angel-number/

Adams, A. (2021b). Pythagorean Numerology: The Full Guide to Modern Numerology. The Sage Divine. https://thesagedivine.com/pythagorean-numerology/

Alex. (2020, October 5). Angel Numbers For Manifestation (Free Angel Numbers & Meanings PDF). Manifest like Whoa! https://manifestlike whoa.com/angel-numbers-manifesting/ #Why_Do_I_Keep_Seeing_Angel_Numbers_After_Manifesting

Angel Number. (2021a). 00 Angel Number – Meaning and Symbolism. Angelnumber.org. https://angelnumber.org/00-angel-number/

Angel Number. (2021b). 000 Angel Number – Meaning and Symbolism. Angelnumber.org. https://angelnumber.org/000-angel-number/

Angel Number. (2021c). 369 Angel Number – Meaning and Symbolism. Angelnumber.org. https://angelnumber.org/369-angel-number-meaning-and-symbolism/

Angel Number. (2021d). 0000 Angel Number – Meaning and Symbolism. Angelnumber.org. https://angelnumber.org/0000-angel-number/

Angel Number. (2021e). Angel Number. Angel Number. https:// angelnumber.org/

Angelou, M. (2021). Still I Rise by Maya Angelou | Poetry Foundation. Poetry Foundation. https://www.poetryfoundation.org/poems/46446/still-i-rise

Bailey, M. (2019, February 20). 8 Ways to Connect With God's Angels. Beliefnet.com. https://www.beliefnet.com/inspiration/angels/galleries/8-ways-to-connect-with-gods-angels.aspx

Beckler, M. (2011, December 25). Steps For Connecting With Angels! Ask-Angels.com. https://www.ask-angels.com/spiritual-guidance/seven-steps-for-connecting-with-your-angels/

Beckler, M. (2016, January 16). Angel Numbers – Learn the Angel Number Meanings Today. Ask-Angels.com. https://www.ask-angels.com/spiritual-guidance/angels-and-numbers/#chapter9

Beech, M. (2020). Discover Your Personality Number. Matt Beech | Mystic. https://mattbeech.com/numerology/personality-number/

Bender, F. (2015, April 12). The Maturity Number. Felicia Bender: The Practical Numerologist. https://feliciabender.com/the-maturity-number/

Bible Gateway. (2019). Psalm 23. Bible Gateway. https://www.biblegateway.com/passage/?search=Psalm%2023&version=NIV

Bontrager, W. (2021). The Energy Represented by Single-Digit Numbers. Affinitynumerology.com. https://affinitynumerology.com/using-numerology/the-energy-represented-by-single-digit-numbers.php

Buddha. (2021). VIMALAKIRTI NIRDESA SUTRA. Kenyon.edu. https://www2.kenyon.edu/Depts/Religion/Fac/Adler/Reln260/Vimalakirti.htm

Carter, L. (2021). method 369: secret code 369 Nikola Tesla write down and get your wishes your desires with the force of energy 3 6 9 (English Edition). Amazon.com. https://www.amazon.com/method-369-secret-desires-English/

Chaplaincy Institute. (2018, August 8). 20 Quotes from the Ancient Scriptures of Hinduism - The Chaplaincy Institute. The Chaplaincy Institute. https://chaplaincyinstitute.org/portfolio-items/20-quotes-from-the-ancient-scriptures-of-hinduism/

Co Manifesting. (2020, August 24). The 3 6 9 Manifestation Technique - Co Manifesting. Co Manifesting. https://comanifesting.com/3-6-9-manifestation-technique/

Davcevski, D. (2016, October 11). The Mindblowing Secret Behind The Numbers 3, 6, and 9 Is Finally Revealed! Life Coach Code. https://www.lifecoachcode.com/2016/10/11/the-secret-behind-3-6-9-revealed/

dCode. (2021). Pythagorean Numerology (Pythagoras Alphabet Number) Online Calculator. Www.dcode.fr. https://www.dcode.fr/pythagorean-numerology

Decoz, H. (2020). Numerology Course: Maturity Number | World

Numerology. Worldnumerology.com. https://www.worldnumerology.com/numerology-Course-15.htm

Dickinson, E. (2014, August 18). "If I can stop one heart from breaking." Daily Poetry. https://dailypoetry.me/emily-dickinson/if-stop-heart-breaking/

Dickinson, E. (2021). "Hope" is the thing with feathers - (314) by... | Poetry Foundation. Poetry Foundation. https://www.poetryfoundation.org/poems/42889/hope-is-the-thing-with-feathers-314

Dilts, C. (2019). 7 Ways to Connect with Your Angels. Learn Religions. https://www.learnreligions.com/how-can-i-connect-with-my-angels-1728995

(2020, December 7). Can Angel Numbers be Two Digits? Numerology Column. https://numerologycolumn.com/can-angel-numbers-be-two-digits/

Ducey, J. (2020, April 6). 555 Manifestation Technique Will Change Your Life. Jake Ducey. https://jakeducey.com/blog/law-of-attraction/555-manifestation/

Duprey, D. (2020, August 17). How To Manifest Anything You Want Using The 5x55 Manifestation Technique. YourTango. https://www.yourtango.com/2020335918/how-manifest-anything-you-want-555-manifestation-technique

Encyclopedia.com. (2013). Fibonacci Sequence. Encyclopedia.com. https://www.encyclopedia.com/science/encyclopedias-almanacs-transcripts-and-maps/fibonacci-sequence

Encyclopedia.com. (2018a). Golden Section. Encyclopedia.com. https://www.encyclopedia.com/science-and-technology/mathematics/mathematics/golden-section

Encyclopedia.com. (2018b). Numerology. Encyclopedia.com. https://www.encyclopedia.com/philosophy-and-religion/other-religious-beliefs-and-general-terms/miscellaneous-religion/numerology

Encyclopedia.com. (2018c). Pythagoras. Encyclopedia.com. https://www.encyclopedia.com/people/philosophy-and-religion/philosophy-biographies/pythagoras

EnlightenmentU Media. (2021a). How To See Angel Numbers? | How Do You See Angel Numbers. EnlightenmentU. https://enlightenmentu.com/how-to-see-angel-numbers-how-do-you-see-angel-numbers/

EnlightenmentU Media. (2021b). When & Who Invented Angel Numbers? |

When & Where Did Angel Numbers Originate? EnlightenmentU Media. https://enlightenmentu.com/when-who-invented-angel-numbers-when-where-did-angel-numbers-originate/

EnlightenmentU Media. (2021c, March 6). Why Have I Stopped Seeing Angel Numbers? EnlightenmentU. https://enlightenmentu.com/i-stopped-seeing-angel-numbers/

Faragher, A. K. (2020, April 10). Numerology 101: How to Calculate Life Path & Destiny Numbers. Allure. https://www.allure.com/story/numerology-how-to-calculate-life-path-destiny-number

Fritscher, L. (2021). How the Collective Unconscious Is Tied to Dreams, Beliefs, and Phobias. Verywell Mind. https://www.verywellmind.com/what-is-the-collective-unconscious-2671571

Frost, R. (2016). The Road Not Taken by Robert Frost | Poetry Foundation. Poetry Foundation. https://www.poetryfoundation.org/poems/44272/the-road-not-taken

Gies, F. C. (1998). Fibonacci | Biography & Facts. In Encyclopædia Britannica. https://www.britannica.com/biography/Fibonacci

Giesemann, S. (2021, February 26). Spirit Communication with Suzanne Giesemann, mystic and medium. Suzanne Giesemann. https://www.suzannegiesemann.com/spirit-connections/

Greater Minds. (2015, June 15). Law Of Attraction Exercises. The Law of Attraction. https://www.thelawofattraction.com/law-of-attraction-exercises/

Greater Minds. (2016, August 24). The Law Of Attraction - Discover How to Improve Your Life. The Law of Attraction. https://www.thelawofattraction.com/

Grey, K. (2016, April 11). The Universe Is Recruiting You! Kyle Gray Explains Angel Numbers And Signs From Above. Www.healyourlife.com. https://www.healyourlife.com/the-universe-is-recruiting-you-kyle-gray-explains-angel-numbers-and-signs-from-above

Hanley, K. (2020, June 23). How Nikola Tesla's 3,6,9 Method Can Change Your Life. Medium; Medium. https://medium.com/@manifestationmagic177/how-nikola-teslas-3-6-9-method-can-change-your-life-f7894fd69025

Helena, D. (2019, December 19). I Stopped Seeing Angel Numbers - Why?

Basically Wonderful. https://www.basicallywonderful.com/stopped-seeing-angel-numbers/

Henley, W. E. (2021). Invictus by William Ernest Henley | Poetry Foundation. Poetry Foundation. https://www.poetryfoundation.org/poems/51642/invictus

Hidden Numerology. (2019 – 2021). Hidden Numerology. https://hiddennumerology.com

Hopkins, G. M. (2020). God's Grandeur by Gerard Manley Hopkins | Poetry Foundation. Poetry Foundation. https://www.poetryfoundation.org/poems/44395/gods-grandeur

Hughes, L. (2021). Dreams by Langston Hughes | Poetry Foundation. Poetry Foundation. https://www.poetryfoundation.org/poems/150995/dreams-5d767850da976

Hunt, T. (2018, December 5). The Hippies Were Right: It's All about Vibrations, Man! Scientific American Blog Network. https://blogs.scientificamerican.com/observations/the-hippies-were-right-its-all-about-vibrations-man/

Hurst, K. (2019, May 23). Angel Numbers Guide: Why You Keep Seeing Angel Number Sequences. The Law of Attraction. https://www.thelawofattraction.com/angel-number-guide/

In5D. (2009, April 19). Number Sequences From Our Spirit Guides. In5D. https://in5d.com/number-sequences-from-our-spirit-guides/

Life Path Number. (2020, June 17). The Connection Between Manifestation And Numerology. Life Path Number. https://lifepathnumber.co/connection-between-manifestation-and-numerology/

Longfellow, H. W. (2021). A Psalm of Life by Henry Wadsworth Longfellow | Poetry Foundation. Poetry Foundation. https://www.poetryfoundation.org/poems/44644/a-psalm-of-life

Manifesting Essentials. (2017). Numerology – Manifesting Essentials. Manifestingessentials.com. http://manifestingessentials.com/numerology-2017/

Mann, A. (2019, November 25). Phi: The Golden Ratio. Live Science. https://www.livescience.com/37704-phi-golden-ratio.html

Meder, A. L. (2014, December 11). Amanda Linette Meder. Amanda Linette Meder; Primal Language Productions LLC. https://www.amandalinet

temeder.com/blog/2014/12/11/10-steps-to-welcome-angels-into-your-home

Miller, L. (2016, November 22). Pythagoras On Human Consciousness. Truth Theory. https://truththeory.com/pythagoras-human-consciousness/

Miller, M. (2012). Rashbi: Basic Kabbalah Tenets. Chabad-Lubavitch Media Center. https://www.chabad.org/kabbalah/article_cdo/aid/380345/jewish/Rashbi-Basic-Kabbalah-Tenets.htm

Monae, S. (2020). HOW TO: 2X22 MANIFESTATION METHOD USING SCRIPTING TO MANIFEST MONEY | MUST SEE RESULTS! [Video]. In YouTube. https://www.youtube.com/watch?v=MKaM8oF6H8E&t=410s

Nayer, D. S., & Zimmer, R. (2007). Deciphering Nature's Code. Chabad-Lubavitch Media Center. https://www.chabad.org/library/article_cdo/aid/463900/jewish/Deciphering-Natures-Code.htm

Nguyen, N. (2018, April 12). Fibonacci and Numerology in Kabbalah; The Tree of Life. Star Tower Heaven Bound. https://modernphilosophystandards.com/2018/04/12/fibonacci-and-numerology-in-kabbalah-the-tree-of-life/

Nothingam, S. (2013, September 25). 10 Feng Shui Tips For A Happy And Harmonious Home. Decoist; Decoist. https://www.decoist.com/2013-09-25/feng-shui-tips/?edg-c=1

Numerology Nation. (2020a, May 27). 3 Secrets Of Angel Number 6: Why You Seeing It? - Numerology Nation. Numerology Nation. https://numerologynation.com/angel-number-6/

Numerology Nation. (2020b, May 28). 3 Secrets Of Angel Number 9: Are You Really Lucky? - Numerology Nation. Numerology Nation. https://numerologynation.com/angel-number-9/

Numerology Nation. (2020c, June 29). Angel Number 4: Is It Really Unlucky? - Numerology Nation. Numerology Nation. https://numerologynation.com/angel-number-4/

Numerology Nation. (2020d, September 1). 11 Secrets Of Angel Numbers: The Complete Guide 2020 - Numerology Nation. Numerology Nation. https://numerologynation.com/angel-numbers-guide/

Numerology Nation. (2021a, February 24). 7 Secrets Why You Are Seeing 3 – The Meaning Of 3 - Numerology Nation. Numerology Nation. https://numerologynation.com/angel-number-3/

Numerology Nation. (2021b, March). 5 Reasons Why You Are Seeing 7 – The Meaning Of 7 - Numerology Nation. Numerology Nation. https://numerologynation.com/angel-number-7/

Numerology Nation. (2021c, March 3). 7 Secrets Why You Are Seeing 1 – The Meaning Of 1 - Numerology Nation. Numerology Nation. https://numerologynation.com/angel-number-1/

Numerology Nation. (2021d, March 5). 5 Secrets Why You Are Seeing 5 – The Meaning Of 5 - Numerology Nation. Numerology Nation. https://numerologynation.com/angel-number-5/

Numerology Nation. (2021e, March 9). 7 Secrets Why You Are Seeing 2 – The Meaning Of 2 - Numerology Nation. Numerology Nation. https://numerologynation.com/angel-number-2/

Numerology Nation. (2021f, March 11). 5 Signs Why You Are Seeing 8 – The Meaning Of 8 - Numerology Nation. Numerology Nation. https://numerologynation.com/angel-number-8/

Numerology Staff. (2021). Angel Numbers: Repeating Number Sequences in Numerology. Numerology.com. https://www.numerology.com/articles/about-numerology/angel-number-meanings/

Padre. (2017, October 10). Angel Numbers. Padre. https://www.guardian-angel-reading.com/blog-of-the-angels/angel-numbers/?media=BLOG&campaign=angel-numbers

Pan, M. (2020, March 27). Numerology Basics: The Ultimate Beginner's Guide. Exemplore - Paranormal. https://exemplore.com/fortune-divination/Numerology-Basics-The-Ultimate-Beginners-Guide

Pearce, J. (2015, February 26). Mindbodygreen. https://www.mindbodygreen.com/0-17567/5-ways-to-connect-with-your-guardian-angel.html

Poetry Foundation. (2013). Gerard Manley Hopkins. Poetry Foundation. https://www.poetryfoundation.org/poets/gerard-manley-hopkins

Psychic Elements. (2017, May 2). The Magic Energy of Numbers. Psychic Elements - Psychics Blog. https://psychicelements.com/blog/the-magic-energy-of-numbers/

Rampton, J. (2015, November 24). 8 Ways to Improve Sleep by Enhancing Your Dreams. Entrepreneur. https://www.entrepreneur.com/article/252743

Sacred Angel Numbers. (2017a). Meaning of Angel Number 11 - Sacred Angel

Numbers. Sacred Angel Numbers. https://www.sacredangelnumbers. com/angel-number-11/

Sacred Angel Numbers. (2017b). Meaning of Angel Number 22 - Sacred Angel Numbers. Sacred Angel Numbers. https://www.sacredangelnum bers.com/angel-number-22/

Sacred Angel Numbers. (2017c). Meaning of Angel Number 44 - Sacred Angel Numbers. Sacred Angel Numbers. https://www.sacredangelnumbers. com/angel-number-44/

Sacred Angel Numbers. (2017d). Meaning of Angel Number 55 - Sacred Angel Numbers. Sacred Angel Numbers. https://www.sacredangelnum bers.com/angel-number-55/

Sacred Angel Numbers. (2017e). Meaning of Angel Number 66 - Sacred Angel Numbers. Sacred Angel Numbers. https://www.sacredangelnumbers. com/angel-number-66/

Sacred Angel Numbers. (2017f). Meaning of Angel Number 77 - Sacred Angel Numbers. Sacred Angel Numbers. https://www.sacredangelnumbers. com/angel-number-77/

Sacred Angel Numbers. (2017g). Meaning of Angel Number 88 - Sacred Angel Numbers. Sacred Angel Numbers. https://www.sacredangelnum bers.com/angel-number-88/

Sacred Angel Numbers. (2017h). Meaning of Angel Number 99 - Sacred Angel Numbers. Sacred Angel Numbers. https://www.sacredangelnum bers.com/angel-number-99/

Sacred Angel Numbers. (2017i). Meaning of Angel Number 111 - Sacred Angel Numbers. Sacred Angel Numbers. https://www.sacredangelnum bers.com/angel-number-111/

Sacred Angel Numbers. (2017j). Meaning of Angel Number 222 - Sacred Angel Numbers. Sacred Angel Numbers. https://www.sacredangelnum bers.com/angel-number-222/

Sacred Angel Numbers. (2017k). Meaning of Angel Number 333 - Sacred Angel Numbers. Sacred Angel Numbers. https://www.sacredangelnum bers.com/angel-number-333/

Sacred Angel Numbers. (2017l). Meaning of Angel Number 444 - Sacred Angel Numbers. Sacred Angel Numbers. https://www.sacredangelnum bers.com/angel-number-444/

Sacred Angel Numbers. (2017m). Meaning of Angel Number 555 - Sacred

Angel Numbers. Sacred Angel Numbers. https://www.sacredangelnum bers.com/angel-number-555/

Sacred Angel Numbers. (2017n). Meaning of Angel Number 777 - Sacred Angel Numbers. Sacred Angel Numbers. https://www.sacredangelnum bers.com/angel-number-777/

Sacred Angel Numbers. (2017o). Meaning of Angel Number 888 - Sacred Angel Numbers. Sacred Angel Numbers. https://www.sacredangelnum bers.com/angel-number-888/

Sacred Angel Numbers. (2017p). Meaning of Angel Number 999 - Sacred Angel Numbers. Sacred Angel Numbers. https://www.sacredangelnum bers.com/angel-number-999/

Sacred Angel Numbers. (2020a). Meaning of Angel Number 1. Sacred Angel Numbers. https://www.sacredangelnumbers.com/angel-number-1/

Sacred Angel Numbers. (2020b). Meaning of Angel Number 2 - Sacred Angel Numbers. Sacred Angel Numbers. https://www.sacredangelnumbers. com/angel-number-2/

Sacred Angel Numbers. (2020c). Meaning of Angel Number 3 - Sacred Angel Numbers. Sacred Angel Numbers. https://www.sacredangelnumbers. com/angel-number-3/

Sacred Angel Numbers. (2020d). Meaning of Angel Number 4 - Sacred Angel Numbers. Sacred Angel Numbers. https://www.sacredangelnumbers. com/angel-number-4/

Sacred Angel Numbers. (2020e). Meaning of Angel Number 5 - Sacred Angel Numbers. Sacred Angel Numbers. https://www.sacredangelnumbers. com/angel-number-5/

Sacred Angel Numbers. (2020f). Meaning of Angel Number 6 - Sacred Angel Numbers. Sacred Angel Numbers. https://www.sacredangelnumbers. com/angel-number-6/

Sacred Angel Numbers. (2020g). Meaning of Angel Number 7 - Sacred Angel Numbers. Sacred Angel Numbers. https://www.sacredangelnumbers. com/angel-number-7/

Sacred Angel Numbers. (2020h). Meaning of Angel Number 8 - Sacred Angel Numbers. Sacred Angel Numbers. https://www.sacredangelnumbers. com/angel-number-8/

Sacred Angel Numbers. (2020i, May 3). Meaning of Angel Number 33 - Sacred Angel Numbers. Sacred Angel Numbers. https://www.sacredangel

numbers.com/angel-number-33/

Sacred Angel Numbers. (2020j, May 6). Meaning of Angel Number 666 - Sacred Angel Numbers. Sacred Angel Numbers. https://www.sacredangel numbers.com/angel-number-666/

Sara. (2020a, December 5). Angel Number 3333 Meaning And Its Significance in Life. Awaken Your Soul with Guardian Angels - ANGELNUMBER.ME. https://angelnumber.me/3333-meaning/

Sara. (2020b, December 11). Angel Number 7777 Meaning And Its Significance in Life. Awaken Your Soul with Guardian Angels - ANGELNUMBER.ME. https://angelnumber.me/7777-meaning/

Sara. (2020c, December 14). Angel Number 11 Meaning And Its Significance in Life. Awaken Your Soul with Guardian Angels - ANGELNUMBER.ME. https://angelnumber.me/11-meaning/

Sara. (2020d, December 18). Angel Number 5555 Meaning And Its Significance in Life. Awaken Your Soul with Guardian Angels - ANGELNUMBER.ME. https://angelnumber.me/5555-meaning/

Sara. (2020e, December 26). Angel Number 1 Meaning And Its Significance in Life. Awaken Your Soul with Guardian Angels - ANGELNUMBER.ME. https://angelnumber.me/1-meaning/

Sara. (2020f, December 27). Angel Number 9 Meaning And Its Significance in Life. Awaken Your Soul with Guardian Angels - ANGELNUMBER.ME. https://angelnumber.me/9-meaning/

Sara. (2020g, December 31). Angel Number 8 Meaning And Its Significance in Life. Awaken Your Soul with Guardian Angels - ANGELNUMBER.ME. https://angelnumber.me/8-meaning/

Sara. (2021a, January 2). Angel Number 6 Meaning And Its Significance in Life. Awaken Your Soul with Guardian Angels - ANGELNUMBER.ME. https://angelnumber.me/6-meaning/

Sara. (2021b, January 6). Angel Number 4 Meaning And Its Significance in Life. Awaken Your Soul with Guardian Angels - ANGELNUMBER.ME. https://angelnumber.me/4-meaning/

Sara. (2021c, January 7). Angel Number 3 Meaning And Its Significance in Life. Awaken Your Soul with Guardian Angels - ANGELNUMBER.ME. https://angelnumber.me/3-meaning/

Sara. (2021d, January 10). Angel Number 2 Meaning And Its Significance in Life. Awaken Your Soul with Guardian Angels - ANGELNUMBER.ME.

https://angelnumber.me/2-meaning/

Sara. (2021e, January 13). Angel Number 66 Meaning And Its Significance in Life. Awaken Your Soul with Guardian Angels - ANGELNUMBER.ME. https://angelnumber.me/66-meaning/

Sara. (2021f, January 18). Angel Number 88 Meaning And Its Significance in Life. Awaken Your Soul with Guardian Angels - ANGELNUMBER.ME. https://angelnumber.me/88-meaning/

Sara. (2021g, January 19). Angel Number 77 Meaning And Its Significance in Life. Awaken Your Soul with Guardian Angels - ANGELNUMBER.ME. https://angelnumber.me/77-meaning/

Sara. (2021h, January 22). Angel Number 55 Meaning And Its Significance in Life. Awaken Your Soul with Guardian Angels - ANGELNUMBER.ME. https://angelnumber.me/55-meaning/

Sara. (2021i, January 25). Angel Number 22 Meaning And Its Significance in Life. Awaken Your Soul with Guardian Angels - ANGELNUMBER.ME. https://angelnumber.me/22-meaning/

Sara. (2021j, February 4). Angel Number 9999 Meaning And Its Significance in Life. Awaken Your Soul with Guardian Angels - ANGELNUMBER.ME. https://angelnumber.me/9999-meaning/

Sara. (2021k, February 6). Angel Number 8888 Meaning And Its Significance in Life. Awaken Your Soul with Guardian Angels - ANGELNUMBER.ME. https://angelnumber.me/8888-meaning/

Sara. (2021l, February 8). Angel Number 6666 Meaning And Its Significance in Life. Awaken Your Soul with Guardian Angels - ANGELNUMBER.ME. https://angelnumber.me/6666-meaning/

Sara. (2021m, February 9). Angel Number 4444 Meaning And Its Significance in Life. Awaken Your Soul with Guardian Angels - ANGELNUMBER.ME. https://angelnumber.me/4444-meaning/

Sara. (2021n, February 13). Angel Number 7 Meaning And Its Significance in life. Awaken Your Soul with Guardian Angels - ANGELNUMBER.ME. https://angelnumber.me/7-meaning/

Sara. (2021o, February 16). Angel Number 33 Meaning And Its Significance in Life. Awaken Your Soul with Guardian Angels - ANGELNUMBER.ME. https://angelnumber.me/33-meaning/

Sara. (2021p, February 18). Angel Number 5 Meaning And Its Significance in Life. Awaken Your Soul with Guardian Angels - ANGELNUMBER.ME.

https://angelnumber.me/5-meaning/

Sara. (2021q, February 22). Angel Number 2222 Meaning And Its Significance in Life. Awaken Your Soul with Guardian Angels - ANGELNUMBER.ME. https://angelnumber.me/2222-meaning/

Sara. (2021r, February 24). Angel Number 99 Meaning And Its Significance in Life. Awaken Your Soul with Guardian Angels - ANGELNUMBER.ME. https://angelnumber.me/99-meaning/

Sara. (2021s, March). Angel Number 44 Meaning And Its Significance in Life. Awaken Your Soul with Guardian Angels - ANGELNUMBER.ME. https://angelnumber.me/44-meaning/

Sara. (2021t, March 26). Angel Number 1111 Meaning And Its Significance in Life. Awaken Your Soul with Guardian Angels - ANGELNUMBER.ME. https://angelnumber.me/1111-meaning/

Shanker, A. (2020, May 31). Law of Attraction and Numerology. Medium. https://medium.com/@Amrittashannker/law-of-attraction-and-numerology-105e79b7dfcb

Spirituality Awakening. (2020, June 6). Single Digit Angel Numbers | Angel Numbers. Spirituality Awakening. https://spirituality-awakening.com/2020/06/06/single-digit-angel-numbers/

Suess, A. J. (2021, January 27). What Are Angel Numbers & What Do They All Mean? - Numerology Sign. Numerologysign.com. https://numerologysign.com/angel-number-meanings/

Taphorn, S. (2021). What Are Angel Numbers and What Do They Tell Us? Www.beliefnet.com. https://www.beliefnet.com/inspiration/angels/what-are-angel-numbers-and-what-do-they-tell-us.aspx

TarotLife. (2021, January 6). Meaning of Numbers (0-9) in Numerology & How to Use Them | Tarot Life. Tarot Life Blog. https://www.yourtarotlife.com/blog/numerology/meaning-of-numerology-numbers-and-uses/

Tennyson, L. A. (2021). In Memoriam A. H. H. OBIIT MDCCCXXXIII: 106 by… | Poetry Foundation. Poetry Foundation. https://www.poetryfoundation.org/poems/57829/in-memoriam-a-h-h-obiit-mdcccxxxiii-106

The Aligned Life. (2018, November 26). How To Manifest With Angel Numbers: What Do They Mean? The Aligned Life. https://www.thealignedlife.co/manifest-angel-numbers-what-do-they-mean/

The Editors of Encyclopaedia Britannica. (2021). Numerology. In Encyclopædia Britannica. https://www.britannica.com/topic/numerology

The Editors of Encyclopedia Britannica. (2018a). Pythagorean theorem | Definition & History. In Encyclopædia Britannica. https://www.britannica.com/science/Pythagorean-theorem

The Editors of Encyclopedia Britannica. (2018b). Pythagoras | Biography, Philosophy, & Facts. In Encyclopædia Britannica. https://www.britannica.com/biography/Pythagoras

The Editors of Encyclopedia Britannica. (2019). Fibonacci numbers | mathematics. In Encyclopædia Britannica. https://www.britannica.com/science/Fibonacci-number

The Numerologist Team. (2015, May 6). What is the Soul Urge Number? Here's How To Calculate & Interpret Yours. Numerologist.com. https://numerologist.com/numerology/how-to-calculate-and-interpret-your-soul-urge-number/

The Secret Of The Tarot. (2017, October). ANGEL NUMBER Meanings & Symbolism - ANGEL NUMBERS. The Secret of the Tarot. https://thesecretofthetarot.com/angel-numbers/

The Secret Of The Tarot. (2019, May 20). ANGEL NUMBER 0000 - Seeing 00:00 (0000 Meaning & Symbolism). The Secret of the Tarot. https://thesecretofthetarot.com/angel-number-0000/

Thesleff, H. (1999, July 26). Pythagoreanism. Encyclopedia Britannica. https://www.britannica.com/science/Pythagoreanism#ref559988

Through the Phases. (2020, May 5). How to Manifest in 5 Days with the 5×55 Manifestation Method. Through the Phases. https://www.throughthephases.com/5x55-manifestation-method/

Virtue, D. (2013). Connect with your Angels. Healyourlife.com. https://www.healyourlife.com/connect-with-your-angels

Virtue, D., & Brown, L. (2004). Angel Numbers Number Sequences From The Angels Doreen Virtue. Mojan.com. https://www.mojan.com/content/angel-numbers-doreen-virtue/

Walmsley, J. (2020). ANGEL NUMBERS - Joanne Sacred Scribes: INDEX - The NUMBERS. ANGEL NUMBERS - Joanne Sacred Scribes. http://sacredscribesangelnumbers.blogspot.com/p/index-numbers.html

Walmsley, J. (2021a, April 2). NUMBER 0. Blogspot.com. http://numerology-thenumbersandtheirmeanings.blogspot.com/2011/05/number-0.html

Walmsley, J. (2021b, April 2). NUMBER 1. Blogspot.com. http://numerology-thenumbersandtheirmeanings.blogspot.com/2011/02/number-1.html

Walmsley, J. (2021c, April 2). NUMBER 2. Blogspot.com. http://numerology-thenumbersandtheirmeanings.blogspot.com/2011/02/number-2.html

Walmsley, J. (2021d, April 2). NUMBER 3. Blogspot.com. http://numerology-thenumbersandtheirmeanings.blogspot.com/2011/02/number-3.html

Walmsley, J. (2021e, April 2). NUMBER 4. Blogspot.com. http://numerology-thenumbersandtheirmeanings.blogspot.com/2011/02/number-4.html

Walmsley, J. (2021f, April 2). NUMBER 5. Blogspot.com. http://numerology-thenumbersandtheirmeanings.blogspot.com/2011/03/number-5-ruler-mars-said-to-be.html

Walmsley, J. (2021g, April 2). NUMBER 6. Blogspot.com. http://numerology-thenumbersandtheirmeanings.blogspot.com/2011/05/number-6.html

Walmsley, J. (2021h, April 2). NUMBER 7. Blogspot.com. http://numerology-thenumbersandtheirmeanings.blogspot.com/2011/05/number-7.html

Walmsley, J. (2021i, April 2). NUMBER 8. Blogspot.com. http://numerology-thenumbersandtheirmeanings.blogspot.com/2011/05/number-8.html

Walmsley, J. (2021j, April 2). NUMBER 9. Blogspot.com. http://numerology-thenumbersandtheirmeanings.blogspot.com/2011/05/number-9.html

Wang, Z. (2020). "The Ascent." The Tang of Poetry. Jtwgroup.com. http://jtwgroup.com/tang-of-poetry/

Whittier, J. G. (2020). Don't Quit. Yourdailypoem.com. http://www.yourdailypoem.com/listpoem.jsp?poem_id=1820

Wigington, P. (2019, April 28). Learn About the Basics of Numerology. Learn Religions. https://www.learnreligions.com/the-basics-of-numerology-2561761

Young, A. (2020, July 8). Who Invented Angel Numbers? - Numerology Origins. Subconscious Servant. https://subconsciousservant.com/who-invented-angel-numbers/